For the Library
Lynchburg College
from
A L Rowse

FOUR CAROLINE PORTRAITS

FOUR CAROLINE PORTRAITS

Thomas Hobbes, Henry Marten, Hugh Peters, John Selden

A.L. Rowse

A.L. Rowse

Duckworth

First published in 1993
Gerald Duckworth & Co. Ltd.
The Old Piano Factory
48 Hoxton Square, London N1 6PB
Tel: 071 729 5986
Fax: 071 729 0015

A catalogue record for this book is available
from the British Library

ISBN 0 7156 2460 1

gift

Photoset in North Wales by
Derek Doyle & Associates, Mold, Clwyd
Printed in Great Britain by
Redwood Press Ltd, Melksham

Contents

To
Elizabeth Longford
and
Antonia Fraser
with admiration and affection

Preface

I suspect that none of my Caroline figures would much care to be subsumed under that title, though their activities fell mainly in the time of Charles I and Charles II. Certainly not the more Puritan or Parliamentarian among my characters. Thomas Hobbes, with whom Charles II was on friendly terms, would not have minded; and perhaps Henry Marten, who cared for nobody, would not have cared. I cannot lay claim to a bias in favour of Puritans or Parliamentarians but, oddly enough, my studies of Hugh Peters and Henry Marten have turned out more favourably towards them than is usual.

Today the press is loaded down with academic books on the 'causes' of the Civil War controverting each other, and theses on the various brands of nonsense thought up by political parties and religious sects, Fifth Monarchy men, Ranters, Levellers, Diggers, Muggletonians, what not. The controversies provide some comic relief in the form of academics being rude to each other, without otherwise enlightening the subject for us:

> great argument
> About it and about, but evermore
> Came out by the same door as in they went.

We should much prefer to know what these people made out of it – Puritan pluralists like Cornelius Burgess, Stephen Marshall, Calamy, Nye and the rest of them, who

7

had been so hot in attacking pluralism in the Church, and then shocked the pure Milton by being no better themselves. What precisely did they *make* – we know that the humbug Burgess made a fortune – much more interesting than what they 'thought', or put forward as thought (mostly nonsense). We know that the horrid Hazelrig, the 'honest' Lilburne, the Leveller Wildman all made the most of their chances: we should like to know just what they made and how. A more rewarding subject for research than their nostrums and fads about society.

> When civil fury first grew high
> And men fell out, they knew not why –

this was true of the great majority, though some knew well enough – they were out for power and profit.

As for thought, one doesn't really want research into the thinking of those who can't think; only the reflections of the few elect spirits who *can* have any value. Especially such minds as Selden or Clarendon, Hobbes or even Milton, wrong-headed as he notably was, for he was a man of genius.

I do not claim to throw light on such deep matters, 'causes' and the like – a great deal in human affairs is very silly (look at politics, the world around us!). More rewarding is to look at the happenings of a given time through the actual lives of a few revealing, rather characteristic, individuals. They at any rate are real.

A.L.R.

CHAPTER 1

The Personality of Thomas Hobbes

What kind of man was Hobbes, a most independent and original of English thinkers, the philosopher who owed least of all his thinking to anyone else?

Hitherto his thought has usually been considered in the abstract, divorced from the man – understandably, since Hobbes was a deductive thinker, making a kind of geometry out of his *speculum mentis*. This is rather imperceptive; for, in fact, Hobbes's thinking – especially in regard to man, society, politics, the moral and social phenomena which form the most important area of his thought – was conditioned largely by his own individual psychology and by the events of his time. Croom Robertson, who wrote the best commentary on Hobbes almost a century ago, saw that clearly. 'More than of almost any other philosopher, it can be said of Hobbes that the key to a right understanding of his thought is to be found in his personal circumstances and the events of his time.'[1]

Hobbes was a plebeian, a lower-class man, and this is the clue to him. In an age when foremost thinkers were aristocrats, like Bacon or Lord Herbert of Cherbury, or of good family like Locke, something of Hobbes's origin clings to the man and his thought all through. Where they were

[1] G.C. Robertson, *Hobbes*, v-vi. Robertson had the great advantage that he had studied the Hobbes mss from Chatsworth and Hardwick.

9

polite, Hobbes has a certain roughness, even uncouthness –
though this does not apply to his English style (it does to
his Latin verses), which was perspicuous, epigrammatic,
pointed. It is even amusing that this nominalist's name
should itself indicate something of his character, for Hob or
Hobs was used in his time to mean a rustic, a country
clown. There was little politeness in Hobbes's composition:
he thought most people fools, and said so. He was quite
right, but upper-class people did not say that sort of thing;
perhaps some of their thinkers – then as now – did not even
recognise it.

Hobbes had no illusions; a man of the people, he had the
lowest opinion of mankind in general – he *knew*, had nothing
but contempt for democracy: he thought it led to anarchy,
and was not far wrong. On liberty he would have agreed with
Lenin: 'Liberty? what for?' Hobbes had no humbug or any
respect for the conventional tissues in which sensible men
wrapped up their real opinion of beliefs they knew to be
nonsense. Hobbes said outright, as far as possible, what he
thought. Of course, even he – living in the seventeenth
century when people were killing each other right and left
for their nonsense convictions – had to be careful. He went as
far as to incur some danger, though a timorous man; he had
a nice trick of going through Holy Writ, in which he was very
well read, and showing up contradictions or confusions, that
things didn't really mean what people thought they did (a
'martyr' merely meant a witness, 'baptism' meant just dipping in water, etc.), interpreting scriptural texts in a down-
to-earth fashion, reducing nonsense as near as possible to
commonsense. Nothing high-falutin', or *exalté*, in this man
of the people: he tells us that 'inspiration' – which Puritan
preachers claimed *ad nauseam* – was just being blown up
with wind, like a bladder.

He was independent-minded and obstinate to the point of
being pig-headed. He was not in the same class as John
Wallis as a mathematician, yet he clung to what he thought

his own original contributions to geometry when quite outclassed – and managed to give some doughty controversial blows in return, if dialectical or personal. This was not his field, which was that of moral and social phenomena, the nature of man and the institutions appropriate to it. He was not interested in metaphysical moonshine – in that rather modern, like most modern philosophers; like them, too, he was interested in logic, and definitions, the analysis of words and phrases. His was an analytical mind, singularly modern – except for his style, which was crisp and idiosyncratic: one recognises the man in every sentence he wrote.

The bias of Hobbes's mind was practical and utilitarian – lower-class again. He thought that human nature was so foolish, men for ever quarrelling and fighting, killing each other for no good reason – except of course self-preservation – that the human record was one of such violence and devastation, homicide and catastrophe, immolation of men in millions, power and force mattering most, that they should be forced into order and discipline under authority. For their own sakes, to keep peace and save their very lives. It is not surprising that Hobbes is the English thinker most respected by Marxists. Nor had he any use for dissidents.

It is significant, though it looks paradoxical, that this plebeian should be the most European of English thinkers – far more than Bacon or Locke, Berkeley or John Stuart Mill. Hobbes spent twenty years altogether on the Continent, where he was a close friend of Mersenne and Gassendi; he had met Galileo and knew his disciple, Berigardus; he controverted Grotius and disputed Descartes. Though he had friends and some admirers in England, he was regarded with more respect on the Continent. The leading English thinker between Bacon and Locke – spanning the decades between the Puritan Revolution and that of 1688 (Locke's victory) – Hobbes was never accepted by the aristocratic Royal Society, regarded as too pugnacious and controversial. He was written down by his own university of Oxford, insulted by its Vice-Chancellor, Dean Fell of Christ Church, as 'irritabile illud et vanissimum Malmesburiense animal' (that vain and conceited Malmesbury creature), and animadverted against by its Chancellor, Lord Clarendon. No upper-class man, Hobbes had a good opinion of himself, and wasn't afraid to express it; nor had he their way of conciliating opponents, the humbug of self-deprecation. He didn't much relish being criticised by second-rate minds – he took no notice of the third-rate. Croom Robertson says, 'Few men have so deeply stirred the minds of their fellows': we might gloss on that – few men have so much *upset* them, exposed their preconceptions, shown them to be nonsense, to be largely camouflaged prejudices; he ripped aside the camouflage, sparing nothing. It was very plebeian of him.

They had their revenge: in the last years of his life his works were censored. Though Charles II was personally friendly – he had no more religious belief than Hobbes had – after about the Plague year (some bright minds put the Plague down to the spread of irreligious ideas) – 'nothing more in English from Hobbes's hand that had any political or religious reference was permitted to see the light as long as he lived'. This is why we do not know as well as we might his *Behemoth*, analysing the causes and consequences of the Civil War, besides various other works, controversial or questioning people's preconceptions.

However, what did it matter? His influence was pervasive, for all the divines and orthodox who thought they could answer him: Hobbes gave the most powerful impulse to the growth of Rationalism in the next century. How important this was we may perceive from the fact that to the end of Hobbes's century people were executed for denying the doctrine of the Trinity; even Sir Isaac Newton decades later had to conceal his disbelief. And Hobbes's intellectual impulse went powerfully on with the Utilitarians and Philosophical Radicals of the nineteenth century – hence the Radical Sir William Molesworth's edition of his works.

Hobbes remains, for an elect mind, stimulating to read not only for his thought but for the brilliance of his style (the plebeian wrote with greater elegance than most upper-class writers) – there was even a certain poetry in this earthy, no-nonsense mind. Nor was he without a homely sense of humour. In discussing the ancient right of Old Sarum to return two burgesses to Parliament, though nobody lived there, he says, 'as I rid in sight of it, if I should tell a stranger that knew not what the word burgess meant, he would think it were a couple of rabbits: the place looketh so like a long cony-borough' (rabbit burrow).

So, where most of his contemporaries are dead to us, he is still alive.

I

Thomas Hobbes was born at Malmesbury, 5 April 1588, of a family of glovers, his father a poor parson. (Shakespeare's father was a glover, whose wife, Mary Arden, came of gentle-folk.) John Aubrey, who knew Hobbes longer than anyone, says that the child's birth was hurried from a fright his mother got upon the rumour of Spanish invasion at the time of the Armada. Actually the father was 'one of the ignorant Sir Johns of Queen Elizabeth's time, could only read the prayers and the homilies, and disesteemed learning as not knowing the sweetness of it. He was a choleric man; a parson (who, I think, succeeded him at Westport,) provoked him on purpose at the church-door. So Vicar Hobbes struck him, and was forced to fly for it, and in obscurity, beyond London, died.'

Westport was just outside the west gate of the town. 'Here was, before the late wars, a very pretty church consisting of a nave and two aisles, and a fair spire-steeple with five tunable bells: which, when the town was taken by Sir William Waller, were converted into ordnance, and the church pulled down to the ground. The steeple was higher than that now standing in the borough, which much added to the prospect. The windows were well painted, and in them were inscriptions that declared much antiquity.' This was the kind of thing that happened all over England as the result of the idiocy of the Civil War. Result: works of men's hands, the artists and craftsmen among them, were destroyed all over the country: palaces, castles, manor-houses; churches and their furnishings, sculpture, carvings, brasses, plate, vestments, music; pictures and paintings, archives and manuscripts, books; what not.

This is the background of what Croom Robertson calls 'the passionate political bias of Hobbes's work', and no wonder it was passionate. This characteristic of it has been rather overlooked by people concentrating on the abstract analysis of his thought. But it is present everywhere, his contempt for ordinary people's stupidity that brings down on them superfluous suffering, their congenital quarrelsomeness and bent for fighting. Hobbes said that 'if it were not for the gallows, some men are of so cruel a nature as to take a delight in killing men – more than I should to kill a bird'. Such people exist, if a small minority – and they are enemies of society. Hobbes was a sensitive timorous man physically, kindly disposed, who never raised a hand against anybody; so he was naturally nervous not only of the brutes who may be a minority, but of ordinary human foolery that incurred such consequences. His psychological make-up gave him foresight into the disastrous events that were being unloosed, when ordinary people couldn't see what was coming. They never do. When the disaster came down upon them, Hobbes wasn't going to suffer for their folly: he was one of the first people to leave the country. It was sensible of him to leave them to it.

1. The Personality of Thomas Hobbes

The boy was quite well taught at the little school in the town, and afterwards at a private school kept by a young University fellow, 'a good Grecian, and the first that came into our parts hereabout since the Reformation. He was a bachelor and delighted in his scholar, T.H.'s company, and used to instruct him in the evening till nine o'clock.' Schoolfellows told Aubrey that as a boy Hobbes was gamesome enough, but even then was apt to withdraw himself to get on with his work. With black hair, they called him 'Crow'. He must already have been remarkable, for as a schoolboy he turned Euripides' *Medea* into Latin iambics.

His benevolent uncle, a glover, sent the boy to Oxford at fourteen, where he remained at Magdalen Hall (now part of Hertford College) for the five years 1603-8. Later in life Hobbes spoke ill of the universities and had no good memory of Oxford where, he said, youth 'were debauched to drunkenness, wantonness, gaming, and other vices'. I dare say he was right enough about *l'homme moyen sensuel*; he was always temperate and under control, and it is likely that the poor plebeian disapproved of the idle better-off youth in the ascendant. It was not a good period for the university, before the reforming impulse of Laud as President of St John's, and later as Chancellor, got going in the 1620s and 1630s. Moreover, Magdalen Hall was stuffed with prating Calvinists, whom Hobbes naturally disliked.

He says later in his Latin autobiographical poem that he was not well taught and rather neglected his studies, except for logic in which he was proficient. He took more pleasure in poring over maps of the world in the bookshops. When the most admired poet of the time, Cowley, came to write his Ode to its leading philosopher, it is interesting that he took up this image:

The Baltic, Euxine, and the Caspian,
And slender-limbed Mediterranean,
Seem narrow creeks to thee, and only fit

15

For the poor wretched fisher-boats of wit.
Thy nobler vessel the vast ocean tries
   And nothing sees but seas and skies
   Till unknown regions it descries,
Thou great Columbus of the Golden Lands of new
   philosophies.

It seems that his genius was late in appearing: it was not until forty, rather too late, that he discovered the delights of geometry, which Descartes had been familiar with from a schoolboy. And at the same time Hobbes began to put forth the fruits of his mature reflection on man and society, provoked by events he mistrusted and feared.

This is another clue to Hobbes, another oddity. It was not until middle age that he began to put his thoughts into writing; he then went on, with abnormal stamina – people paid tribute to it – writing original works well into his eighties. All his life he was meditating, thinking things out for himself. He didn't read much; he was apt to say that if he had read as much as other men, he would have known as little as they did. In keeping with Sir Philip Sidney's famous line, he looked within himself and wrote. Aubrey says that he had few books, and 'as for his self-praise, they can have very little skill in morality that cannot see the justice of commending a man's self, as well as of anything else, in his own defence'. Hobbes was conscious of the need to defend himself: he was so original that no one fully understood him, and so comprehensive a thinker that no one could get all round him. Anyhow, as Henry James says: 'Nobody ever understands *any*thing'; one has to explain oneself.

The university over for good and all, Hobbes had the luck to enter into service with the eminent Cavendish family of Chatsworth and Hardwick. Bess of Hardwick's able son, William, had been made Earl of Devonshire and now took on Hobbes as tutor to his son. This youth was something of

16

a waster (unlike his father) and would send Hobbes 'up and down to borrow money, being ashamed to speak himself'. Hobbes kept his purse for him, grew fond of the young lord, much his own age, and went hawking and hunting with him. The Cavendishes were a musical lot, and the young tutor became 'much addicted to music, and practised on the bass-viol'. Even as an old man Hobbes continued his singing, if only to exercise his lungs; he would shut himself in the big turret-room that was his on the leads at Hardwick and sing to himself, disturbing no one and undisturbed. So like him: not at all the morose character he has been made out to be.

His relations with his young master were singularly affectionate, and he so much shared his way of life that he began to forget his Latin. It was just like Hobbes to correct this himself: he took to taking a little Elzevir edition of one of the classics in his pocket, 'particularly Caesar's Commentaries, which he did read in the lobby or ante-chamber while his lord was making his visits'. Together the young men made the tour of France and Italy; it was Hobbes's first initiation into the ways of the Continent, useful for his acquisition of modern languages. We know little about it except that it took place in 1610, the year of the assassination of Henri IV by the fanatic Ravaillac, which had such ill consequences for France. It must have made a lasting impression on Hobbes's mind.

He continued in the Devonshire family after the tutorship as the friend of his lord, who succeeded to the earldom in 1626. At this time they made their peregrination about the Peak, admiring its natural beauties, which Hobbes celebrated in his Latin poem on its Wonders. Two years later the young Earl was dead. Even after half a century Hobbes's Latin verses are touched with pathos at the ending of this friendship: the twenty years of companionship, he said, were by far the sweetest of all his long life, to the end they would come back in dreams.

He owed his introduction to society to his place with the family, and came to know Bacon. This would be in the last years of the great man's life, 1622-6, during his retirement at Gorhambury, when, out of the snake-pit of politics, the philosopher could give himself up to thinking. Aubrey says that Bacon loved to converse with Hobbes, who could understand what he said. Bacon would dictate his thoughts to his young men, but often found that he could not make sense of what ordinary folk wrote down. Not so with Hobbes. Here again the remarkable thing is that Bacon should have had little influence on Hobbes's thinking – one more indication of his extraordinary independence and self-sufficiency. In the event they were almost at opposite poles intellectually: Bacon interested in natural science, scientific experiments and his own kind of inductive method, which Hobbes thought nothing of; Hobbes the analyst, absorbed in deduction from his acute definitions over a wide range of observation, yet essentially a deductive thinker, the geometer of politics and society.

During these years Hobbes read a good many romances and plays – he became a friend of Ben Jonson and the Scots scholar and poet, Sir Robert Aytoun, a kinsman of young Lady Devonshire. He told Aubrey that he regretted all this reading as a waste of time – though Aubrey appreciated that it increased Hobbes's remarkable command and 'copie' (copiousness) of words. More significant was his translation of Thucydides, and his choice of the fountain-head of historical writing. For Thucydides hated democracy and demagogues, and put down the disasters to Athens in the Peloponnesian War to their divisions and conflicts, their natter about politics and their squabbles. Nor had this elect spirit any respect for the 'ridiculous religion' of the common people. Forty years later, Hobbes said that already he had wanted to bring home to his squabbling contemporaries the folly of Athenian democracy, leading to anarchy. 'In Athens no man so poor but was a statesman. So St Luke, Acts

XVII, 21. All the Athenians spend their time in nothing but hearing and telling of news: the true character of politicians without employment.'

It was about this time, not until he was forty, that Hobbes fell in love with geometry – an odd passion to entertain, but it came to possess him, in the absence of more physical endearments. (He remained celibate.) He happened to be in a gentleman's library one day, where 'Euclid's Elements lay open, and 'twas the 47 El. libri l. He read the proposition. 'By God,' said he, 'this is impossible!' So he reads the demonstration of it, which referred him back to such a proposition, which he read. That referred him back to another, which he also read. Et sic deinceps [and so one after another], that at last he was demonstratively convinced of that truth. This made him in love with geometry.'

It was so like him to come to it his own way, and no one else's. This had its disadvantage: autodidacts are apt to be more tenacious of what they have won so hardly. And later Hobbes was convinced that he had made discoveries in this field that was not his own, and hung on to them obstinately even when disproved.

His beloved young lord and friend dead, Hobbes took on the son of a neighbouring Midlands gentleman, Sir Gervase Clinton, for another Continental tour, 1629-31. Again Hobbes tells us nothing of it, but he would have had the opportunity of observing from close at hand Richelieu's reduction of disorder in the French state and the example he set of authoritarian monarchy. While in Paris Hobbes received an invitation to return to the Devonshire family and undertake the education of the boy who was the third Earl. For the next seven years Hobbes instructed him in logic, rhetoric, law – the subjects upon which he was himself meditating to write – and 'with all such opinions as should incline him to be a good Christian, a good subject, and a good son'. The tutor became in effect an

19

indispensable friend of the family, something of a steward, helping with the regulation of the large household that went to and fro between Chatsworth and Hardwick, and London, and formulating their accounts.

He was on no less friendly terms with the Earl of Newcastle, cousin of his own Lord, and head of the junior line of Cavendishes at Welbeck and Bolsover. Newcastle, like some other members of the family, had scientific as well as literary interests. We find Hobbes writing to him at New Year 1634, 'my first business in London was to seek for Galileo's *Dialogues*; at taking my leave of your lordship I undertook to buy it for you, but it is not possible to get it for money ... I hear say it is called in, in Italy, as a book that will do more hurt to their religion than all the books have done of Luther and Calvin, such opposition they think is between their religion and natural reason. I doubt not but the translation of it will here be publicly embraced, and therefore wish extremely that Dr Webbe would hasten it. There is no news at Court but of masques, which is a stay to my Lord's going to Oxford because he is one of the masquers.'

Some months later Hobbes paid his last visit to his native Wiltshire, where Aubrey first saw him. The boy was then at school at Leigh Delamere – now the site of a demotic service station off the M4 – where Hobbes came to visit his old schoolmaster and Aubrey's relations. 'He was then a proper man, brisk, and in very good habit' – this means well set up. 'His hair was then quite black', and rather wavy.

Shortly he set off, with his pupil, on a third Continental tour which lasted a couple of years, 1634-6. From Paris in August 1635 Hobbes wrote to thank Newcastle for a generous gift, a spur to his endeavour. Newcastle was passionately interested in horsemanship, so that we find Hobbes sending back equestrian news and actually writing a pamphlet on the motions of the horse in straight line or circular. More to his mind probably, 'I understand not how Mr Warner[2] will demonstrate those inventions of the multiplying glass and burning glass so infinite in virtue as he pretend ...' Hobbes goes into the issues in detail, then 'I hope your lordship will not bestow much upon the hopes, but suffer the liberal sciences to be liberal ... For the soul I know he has nothing to give your lordship any satisfaction. I would he could give good reasons for the faculties and passions of the soul such as may be expressed in plain English, if he can; he is the first that I ever heard of could speak sense in that subject. If he cannot, I hope to be the first.'

We see what occupied Hobbes's 'working mind' while on the tour, the direction of his interests, and also his self-confidence. 'We are unsettled, I have no time – for going up and down with my Lord – neither for myself, nor for Mydorgius [Mydorge, a friend of Descartes], nor for books. All I study is a nights and that for a little while is the reading of certain new books, especially Mr Selden's *Mare Clausum* and a book of my Lord of Castle Island's concerning truth [Lord Herbert of Cherbury's *De Veritate*], which is a high point, and both these books are new set forth since I came abroad. Mydorgius tells me he has sent to Sir Charles [Cavendish] his treatise of refraction perfected.'

In his next bulletin Hobbes sets forth his view: 'in things that are not demonstrable, of which kind is the greatest part of natural philosophy, as depending upon the motion of bodies so subtle as they are invisible – such as are air and spirits – the most that can be attained unto is to have such opinions as no certain experience can confute, and from which can be deduced by lawful argumentation no absurdity ... For the optics I know Mr Warner and M. Mydorge are as able men as any in Europe, but they do not

[2] Walter Warner, mathematician and natural philosopher.

well to call their writings demonstrations, for the grounds
and suppositions they use – so many of them as concern
light – are uncertain and many of them not true.'

Hobbes continues to discuss their experiments and
hypotheses in detail. Then, turning to Newcastle's personal
affairs and disappointments at Court – 'he that will
venture to sea must resolve to endure all weather, but for
my part I love to keep a' land' – a very Hobbesian
sentiment. He recommends Newcastle to console himself
with meditation, in which he will find 'that happiness
which I and all that are in love with knowledge use to fancy
to themselves for the true happiness in this life'. From
France Hobbes travelled with his young lord through the
Alps to Italy. In Florence he was well received by and
discoursed with Galileo, for whom he always had profound
respect: the man 'that first opened the gate of natural
philosophy universal'. And he saw more of Galileo's leading
disciple, Berigardus. During this time Hobbes's mind was
occupied by the problem of motion: 'whether he sails,
drives, or rides, there motion is for ever meeting his eye',
engaging his thought and offering itself as the clue to the
mystery of the varied universe. The point not clear is when
he first seriously conceived that there was a mystery to
solve, and that he might solve it.' This was when he was
nearing fifty.

In Paris his philosophical interests derived much
encouragement from Père Mersenne, the mathematician
and friend of Descartes, of whose scientific circle Hobbes
was an intimate. Mersenne became a close friend. Hobbes
was well respected in the circle; with Descartes his
relations were ambivalent, Hobbes disagreed on various
points and I dare say he was jealous of Descartes'
mathematical superiority. To Descartes everything had
come early and quickly, with the precocious flash of genius;
Hobbes worked slowly and lumberingly, but with gradually
growing intellectual ambition, to a no less comprehensive

scheme of thought. He would write a treatise, first *De Corpore*, i.e. on Nature; second, *De Homine*, on Man; third, *De Cive*, i.e. on Society. Revolutionary events at home were to throw the scheme out of gear and force him to deal with the last subject first, as most urgent in the crisis that was developing.

It was ambitious of him, and also rather old-fashioned, to think of compassing the whole map of human experience and thought in one system, charting it in accordance with his own independent and self-sufficient ideas, some of them obstinate prejudice or preconceptions he would never give up. 'Hobbes stands apart in his country and his time, a philosopher of large constructive ambition, yet who confined his thought to the world of experience and was moved by the most directly practical purpose.' We must never forget that, when so much emphasis has been laid on the deductive character of his thought, and indeed the method of his reasoning. Paradoxically, in his case his abstract generalisations carry practical point, sometimes a spike. He is a commonsense plebeian, his main concern the practical direction of human conduct – to the end of self-preservation. And at a time when Europe was exhausted and devastated by the Thirty Years' War – Bismarck said that Germany still bore the scars of it two centuries later – and England was indulging in a civil war of her own. Of Hobbes's philosophical scheme forming in his mind Croom Robertson says, 'never did human purpose become more the sport of outer events'. It forced forward an acute concern with politics and the problems of society, which henceforth never left him, relegating other interests to the background.

Arrived back in England in the autumn of 1636, Hobbes writes to Newcastle that, though the Devonshires 'do both accept so well of my service as I could almost engage myself to serve them as a domestic all my life, yet the extreme pleasure I take in study overcomes in me all other appetites'. He bears this out with a long discussion of light and its refraction, basing himself on Galileo but giving his own explanation of the phrases that he uses. Optics were a dominant interest of his in these years. He goes on to describe an experiment for making ice with snow – 'this I have seen'; it takes us back to Bacon's last experiment. One way and another we see that Hobbes was not so uninterested in experimental science, so exclusively deductive a thinker, as is usually thought.

In May 1637 Newcastle was writing to his cousin Devonshire at Chatsworth, 'my service to Mr Hobbes. Pray tell him Mr Warner would make us believe miracles by a glass he can make. I doubt he will prove Ben's Doctor Subtle.' Subtle is Ben Jonson's Alchemist. Walter Warner, Aubrey tells us, was 'both mathematician and philosopher, and 'twas he that put out Thomas Hariot's Algebra'. He also made 'an Inverted Logarithmical Table'; then Aubrey comments sensibly, 'Quaere Dr Pell, what is the use of those Inverted Logarithms?'

We see the intellectual interests of this circle, so rudely interrupted by the Civil War.

Hobbes came back to the gathering clouds at home, to embittered squabbles for which he, as a sensible man, had little but contempt – 'squabblings about free-will and standing upon punctilios concerning the service-book and its rubrics'. So much for Archbishop Laud, whom he regarded as a tactless don to bother about such things. Then there was the rumpus about Ship Money: 'mark the oppression! a Parliament man of £500 a year land-taxed at 20s.' So much for John Hampden, who became a national hero among the gentry for refusing to pay a reasonable demand for the upkeep of the Navy: coastal counties paid it, why shouldn't inland counties, for national defence? It was mere chicken-feed compared with the excise imposed by Parliament to fight their war, the levies upon people by both sides in the course of their fractious conflict. Hobbes saw that each side was heading for a clash, though even he could hardly have foreseen how ghastly a catastrophe it would be. Some people on both sides, as usual enough with humans, were spoiling for a fight.

Hobbes told Aubrey that 'at his Lord's house in the country there was a good library and books enough for him, and that his lordship stored the library with what books he thought fit to be bought. But the want of learned conversation was a very great inconvenience, and, though he conceived he could order his thinking as well perhaps as another man, yet he found a great defect.' So far from being unsociable, he had a wide circle of friends and much enjoyed the conversation of Mersenne's acquaintance in Paris. In London Hobbes was friendly with Ben Jonson and Aytoun, Selden, Waller, Davenant, Dr Harvey, and members of Falkland's circle, who was 'his great friend and admirer'. With him he would have met Sidney Godolphin, the Cavalier poet, who was to be killed in the Civil War and left Hobbes a legacy of £100. To his memory Hobbes dedicated *Leviathan*: 'when he lived, he was pleased to think my studies something and otherwise to oblige me with real testimonies of his good opinion, great in themselves and the greater for the worthiness of his person.' Selden and Harvey also left Hobbes small legacies, testimonials of friendship.

Civil War was portended – indeed ultimately initiated – by the rebellion in Scotland against the introduction of an attractive service-book following the model of the Anglican liturgy. Charles I and Laud had no idea of the explosion it would give rise to – the swearing of a National Covenant, the raising of an army; Scottish nobles connived at it, and took the lead in order to be 'with it' for their own self-interest as at the original Reformation of John Knox. Now another intriguing minister, Alexander Henderson, took the lead in Covenant and propaganda. One gets the impression that the Scots too were spoiling for a fight;

Charles I's two ineffective campaigns – the 'Bishops' Wars' – were sabotaged by the gentry in general, gathering momentum against Charles's régime. This precipitated the calling of Parliament. The fat was in the fire.

Hobbes – more sensitive and far-sighted than most – was fearful of the outcome. Anxious to put forward his diagnosis of the trouble, he put aside his larger systematic work to concentrate on the political issue. He wrote 'a little treatise in English' to show that the Crown's rights, now called in question by Parliament, were inseparably a part of sovereignty, and that no one denied that sovereignty lay in the king. Though not printed, the work was circulated, 'many gentlemen had copies, which occasioned much talk of the author and – had not his Majesty dissolved the Parliament [the Short Parliament of 1640], it had brought him into danger of his life'. This episode has usually been discounted, and Hobbes may have exaggerated his danger; but indeed several people were sent to the Tower or imprisoned for less, such was the temper of Parliament. Hobbes was right to leave the country for the fighting fools to fight it out.

II

Hobbes was sure of a welcome in Paris, especially in Mersenne's circle and by Gassendi, best of men, of whom he became an intimate friend. Gassendi was an exponent of the atomic theory of Epicurus, and a critic of Descartes who was living in Holland. Mersenne forwarded some sixteen objections to different points in Descartes' philosophical *Meditationes* without giving Hobbes's name, who had already compared certain of Descartes' hypotheses in physics with his own conclusions. Descartes spotted that the anonymous critic was more interested in elaborating Hobbes's own independent position than in Descartes' philosophising: this vexed him and he did not pursue the correspondence. When *De Cive* was printed Descartes suspected a common hand in that and the critic of his views, and said that Hobbes's ability in morals and politics was greater than in physics and metaphysics – which was no doubt the case.

Hobbes took with him his total capital of £500 to live on, but said that his absence abroad cost him some thousands in all. For he stayed away for eleven years – through revolution, civil war raging up and down the country, killing of friends; through Scottish invasions, rebellion in Ireland, imposition of the Scotch Covenant (which turned out a dud); reduction of Parliament to a mere Rump, execution of the King, the erection of a republic under the name of a Commonwealth. In a letter to Devonshire in 1641 he wrote, in regard to the attack on episcopacy and the Church, that 'experience teaches thus much, that the dispute between the spiritual and the civil power has of late, more than any other thing in the world, been the cause of civil wars in all places of Christendom'. The Thirty Years' War between Counter-Reformation and militant Protestantism was still devastating Germany, and France continued to enjoy religious dissensions though Richelieu had suppressed the Huguenot power to challenge the state. Hobbes's resolution of the problem was the complete subordination of religion to the state – nothing else, he was sure, would be effective.

In 1642 his pupil, Devonshire, was impeached for joining the King at York, expelled from the House of Lords and ordered to the Tower. Instead, he left for abroad, when his estates were sequestrated. In 1645 he made his peace with the victorious Parliament, paid an enormous fine and was allowed home to live in retirement. In 1643 his uncle, Sir Charles Cavendish – the gifted mathematician who appears in Hobbes's correspondence – was killed at Gainsborough. He was forced by Cromwell's charge into a quagmire, where 'one officer cut him on the head',

Cromwell reported with satisfaction, 'and, as he lay, my captain-lieutenant Berry thrust him into the short ribs, of which he died about two hours after in Gainsborough'. This same year two more friends were killed; Lord Falkland at Newbury and Sidney Godolphin in the West.

The intervention of the Presbyterian Scots turned the scales against the Royalist cause, and after the disaster of Marston Moor, where Newcastle had been in command, he too left the country and joined the exiles, for a time, in Paris. There the circle could to some extent reconstitute itself. The magnificent Newcastle, who had spent a fortune on the King's cause, was reduced to living on credit – at one time Hobbes lent him £90 – but continued to entertain him at his table, along with Gassendi who had been a correspondent of Sir Charles Cavendish, to whom Descartes had dedicated a book.

The distracting events in England forced Hobbes to lay aside his scientific interests and urged him powerfully towards the problems of politics and society. *De Cive*, written in Latin for the benefit of European opinion, appeared in 1642; in 1647 it came out in fuller form at Amsterdam, with answers to objections on various points, and a Preface explaining its place in his general philosophical scheme and why it was forced out of due order. In 1646 Hobbes paid a visit to Rouen, another centre of English exiles, where he wrote his tract 'Of Liberty and Necessity', which provoked controversy as usual when published some years later. He had an admirer in a gentleman of Languedoc, Du Verdus, who almost per-suaded him to take up residence with him in the South, so hopeless seemed the posture of affairs in England. Hobbes was dissuaded from this step by the appearance of the Prince of Wales in Paris; Newcastle had been his Governor, and it may have been he who recommended Hobbes as mathematical tutor to the Prince. Hobbes's personality recommended itself to the young man, as it did to so many;

later, his intellectual influence upon him, if any, decidedly heterodox as it was, was thought to be deleterious by the orthodox. Charles II had little religious belief, but privately gave the benefit of the doubt to the Church of Rome.

Hobbes, like the Erastian he was, gave the benefit of the doubt to the established Church of England. In 1647 he was dangerously ill at St Germain and thought not likely to recover. Père Mersenne came to what he thought was his death-bed, hoping to reconcile him at the last to Rome. Hobbes interrupted: 'Father, I have debated all that with myself long ago, and have no mind to discuss it now. You can entertain me better: when did you see Gassendi?' It was the priest who shortly died. Hobbes unexpectedly got better, but he did not object to the prayers of Dr Cosin who adhered to the Prayer Book – after all, the Church of England was the state church.

With all the English exiles gathering in France Hobbes had plenty of company among his own countrymen. John Evelyn, for one, knew him well there, and has left a note of an interesting occasion in his Diary. One day in September 1651, 'I went to visit Mr Hobbes the famous philosopher of Malmesbury, with whom I had long acquaintance: from whose window we saw the whole equipage and glorious cavalcade of the young French monarch, Louis XIV, passing to Parliament, when first he took the kingly government on him.' The spectacle must have given Hobbes some reflexions on his own country.

All this while he was shaping up his *magnum opus* on politics, *Leviathan, or the Matter, Form, and Power of a Commonwealth Ecclesiastical and Civil*. Into it he put all his observation of and insight into the ruinous experience of his time. Never was a work of thought deductive in form so much influenced by events. As Croom Robertson emphasises, Hobbes had an urgent message to deliver; 'the practical interest was always uppermost in him': he saw that society was in danger of anarchy unless controlled by strong authoritarian government. In the privacy of one's own mind one could think what one liked (he certainly did); but for the sake of the overwhelming necessity of peace and order one should conform outwardly and obey. This message has not lost its relevance today; its force depends on the degree of disorder, the danger of anarchy which a particular society suffers. One can certainly see its relevance to Communist societies. No wonder Thomas Hobbes is more appreciated by Marxists; the English mind has usually suffered from complacency – Hobbes had no sympathy with that state of mind.

In England Parliament's victory had been decisive, brought home to the world by the trial and execution of the King – Milton boasted to Europe of the public nature of the demonstration – and the erection of a republic. There seemed no further hope for the Royalists; even the Duke of Buckingham, who had been brought up with the royal children, advised Newcastle, 'the best counsel that I am able to give you, considering the present state of our affairs, is to make your peace, if it be possible, in England.' Newcastle could not do so, he had been proclaimed traitor and excepted from all pardon. But Hobbes had not taken up arms against Parliament, and his branch of the family, the Devonshires, were now living peaceably under its rule.

He said lightly that he 'had a mind to go home', and this was held against him by the critics to whom he was always exposed. There were good reasons why he should go home. Probably his money was running out; more important, when *Leviathan* was published in 1651, its open attack on the record of the Roman Church in history, its constant meddling in politics and stirring up civil dissension, with derogatory remarks about the Papacy, exposed him to more danger in France now than he would meet with in England. He had no mind to be caught for exposing their superstitions by people whose intelligence he despised: England was safer for an attack on Rome – and safety was an unquestionable good when so many people were killing each other for their 'convictions'.

He gives a clue to his state of mind in his Latin autobiographical poem when he says that he had Dorislaus and Ascham in mind. Dorislaus, ambassador of the new Commonwealth, had been assassinated at the Hague in 1649, and Ascham, envoy to Spain, in Madrid in 1650. Such were the amenities of civil war extending its dangers abroad, or, as Hobbes put it, such was the fear awaiting the proscribed everywhere:

Tanquam proscripto terror ubique aderat.

Now an old man – for the time – of sixty-four, he made up his mind to return. Before doing so he responded to the appeal of his friend Davenant, who had narrowly escaped execution, to give his judgment on the subject of heroic poetry, *à propos* of the Preface to Davenant's example of the *genre*, his large-scale *Gondibert*. Hobbes obliged with polite praise of the poem, which was generally admired and, while disclaiming literary criticism, characteristically laid about him. Though some heathen poets 'had the name of prophets', the best of them were at least free from the 'indiscretions' of seventeenth-century divines. Fancy was really memory, so 'her voyage was not very great, herself being all she seeks'.

On Hobbes's return to London he lived at first in Fetter Lane, for the sake of company and intellectual discourse – Aubrey tells us that he was much sought after. He was now a famous figure, but the Commonwealth or, after 1653, Protectorate, apprehended no trouble from him: the whole argument of *Leviathan* was in favour of accepting a *de facto* government once it was strong enough to establish order and command obedience. It was the Royalists who were scandalised now, and from that time attacks rained upon him from this quarter. For the remainder of his long life he was involved in controversy: it was usually *Leviathan* that was attacked, then too his views on Free-Will and religion, and no less his obstreperous and wrong-headed contributions to the delights of geometry. It must be admitted that in this field he took the offensive and gave provocation – perhaps in others too – and was obstinate into his eighties. It was very exceptional that he should have written important works as an octogenarian; he even translated the whole of the *Iliad* and *Odyssey* into English verse in his middle eighties.

About 1653 he returned to living off and on with the Devonshire family, in London at Little Salisbury House and in the country at Chatsworth and Hardwick when they returned to their estates. Aubrey tells us that he wrote a long Latin poem about 'the encroachment of the clergy, both Roman and Reformed, on the civil power. I remember he did read Cluverius' *Historia Universalis* and made up his poem from thence ... His place of meditation was then in the portico in the garden. He would set his thoughts upon researching and contemplating, always with this rule that he deeply considered one thing at a time, *scilicet*, a week or sometimes a fortnight.' Concentration was the key to his prodigious output. In this way, having delivered his message on the most urgent need of the time – internal peace and order – he was able to go back to the foundations of his ambitious scheme and produce his book on Nature, *De Corpore*, in 1655 and on Man, *De Homine*, in 1658.

Foreign visitors were quite as anxious to meet the ageing philosopher as they were Milton, notorious for his defence of the King's execution – indeed more so, for Hobbes was far more famous. His portrait was demanded, and Samuel Cooper, 'our common friend, the prince of limners, drew his picture as like as art could afford: which his Majesty at his return bought of him and conserves as one of his great rarities in his closet at Whitehall.'

How would he be received by his former pupil, now that

he was disapproved of by the Royalists who suspected that he had instilled heterodox notions into Charles II's head? Aubrey tells us: 'about two or three days after his Majesty's happy return, as he was passing in his coach through the Strand, Mr Hobbes was standing at Little Salisbury House gate, where his Lord then lived. The King spied him, put off his hat very kindly to him and asked him how he did. About a week after he had oral conference with his Majesty at Mr Samuel Cooper's, where, as he sat for his picture, he was diverted by Mr Hobbes's pleasant discourse. Here his Majesty's favours were redintegrated to him, and order was given that he should have free access to his Majesty, who was always much delighted in his wit and smart repartee.' All was well with the easy-going, cynical King; not with the orthodox and unco' guid however.

At Court the clever young men would bait the old man, who gave as good as he got. 'Here comes the Bear to be baited!' the merry monarch would say. The polemicist was very ready with his repartees, 'and that without rancour, except provoked'. Naturally his manners would not have the smooth disingenuousness of courtiers, any more than Clarendon's had. He did not take them seriously; if they expected a serious answer to a mathematical problem 'he turned and winded and compounded in philosophy, politics, etc, as if he had been at analytical work. He always avoided, as much as he could, to conclude hastily.'

We must not involve ourselves in the controversies in which Hobbes involved himself, merely notice them as occupying so much of his life from this time forward. He was already at issue with Bishop Bramhall on the subject of Free Will, so much to the fore with the Calvinist insistence upon Predestination – whole libraries written on this non-sense subject. ('Have you ever *met* a determinist?', said a young Oxford philosopher of today, much to the point.) Hobbes's personal shafts reveal him: 'I have been publicly injured by many of whom I took no notice, supposing that that humour would spend itself; but, seeing it last and grow higher, I thought it necessary at last to make of some of them, and first of this bishop, an example.' In the reaction brought about by the Restoration, however, attacks on the score of impiety and blasphemy, insinuations as to atheism, had their danger.

In November 1661 we find Mr Pepys, after a busy day in Westminster, at home in bed 'and lay long reading Hobbes's *Liberty and Necessity*, a little but very shrewd piece, and so to sleep'. But shortly Hobbes felt obliged to appeal to the King's protection. A general amnesty had been proclaimed at the Restoration; he had not attacked episcopacy, though the bishops attacked him regularly in their sermons. It was true that he made the authority of the Church dependent on royal power – 'which I hope your Majesty will think is neither atheism nor heresy.' There was no ground for calumny in his writings – 'there is no sign of it in my life.' It was rather provoking to his enemies that the conduct of his life gave them no ammunition against him: all agreed that it was disciplined, temperate and blameless. 'And for my religion, when I was at the point of death at St Germain, the Bishop of Durham [Cosin] can bear witness of it, if he be asked.' He asked the King not to 'believe so ill of me upon reports that proceed often from the displeasure which commonly ariseth from difference in opinion'.

Ironically as it seems for one who preached absolutism in sovereign power (since Charles II agreed with him), the atmosphere grew increasingly hostile, and from this time dates the disparagement and depreciation with which the most original of political thinkers in the English tradition came to be treated. But he was not traditional, as the Whig John Locke was, who came to be far more influential. Privately, Charles II agreed with Hobbes about sovereignty, and largely about religion; but those who agreed with Hobbes's heterodox views could not come into the open to defend him: he became the founder of English Deism, which surfaced in the next century. Meanwhile, Pepys tells us in 1668, on 3rd September – the day of Cromwell's victories – that he called at several businesses, 'and particularly my bookseller's for Hobbes's *Leviathan*, which is now mightily called for; and what was heretofore sold for 8s, I now give 24s, for at the second-hand it is sold for 30s – it being a book the bishops will not let be printed again.'

Hobbes had a wish to see a free school founded in his native town and was willing to help, as also to persuade the King to donate a piece of land to provide the headmaster's salary. Here too he was frustrated: 'the Queen's priests, smelling out the design and being his enemies, hindered this public and charitable intention.' Obstinately Hobbes continued to hold the low opinion of university education he had formed from his own experience sixty years before. In part he was mistaken, for the universities had changed greatly in the interval and were the home of brilliant talents, particularly in the scientific sphere. On the other hand, nothing changed his view that studying the classical authors encouraged irresponsible ideas of liberty and disorder, dislike of authority if not positive sedition. (Ironically again, the career of his greatest successor, John Locke, would bear him out.) It was hardly surprising therefore that Hobbes was now under attack from both Oxford and Cambridge.

A distinguished group of scientists had gathered together at Oxford, from which the Royal Society took its rise, and they were friends. Boyle was the leading experimenter, but also deeply religious; Seth Ward was a good mathematician, on his way to becoming a bishop; John Wallis, a recruit from Cambridge, was the most brilliant mathematician. The ageing philosopher got into controversy with each of them: by this time he had fixed ideas on mathematics and was convinced that he had original contributions to make. So he may have had, but they were wrong-headed, and in his prolonged controversies with Wallis he was worsted on the mathematical points in question. It was not like Hobbes to give up; he could still score dialectical points, and Wallis had an Achilles' heel: he had deciphered Charles I's secret papers captured at Naseby, used in evidence against him by Parliament. Hobbes did not let him off that hook – perhaps all the more because he was convinced that Wallis and his friends kept him out of the Royal Society. Hobbes submitted three papers to this august, if by no means exclusive, body: it was not nice for the most famous thinker in England to be excluded by people most of whom were third-rate, and he resented it. He knew his own value, and was not afraid to state it when forced to do so – as he said of Bishop Bramhall: 'What my works are he was no fit judge. But now he has provoked me, I will say this much of them: neither he, if he had lived, nor I, if I would, could extinguish the light which is set up in the world by the greatest part of them.'

This was very grand, but it was true: to Europe he was the leading English thinker of his time.

Nevertheless, censored as he was, he held on his way. It is remarkable that in his last years, besides all the sterile controversies, he completed three substantive works: a work on the Elements of Law, which has been edited and given its proper shape only in our own time; his *Historia Ecclesiastica*; and *Behemoth*, his account of the causes of the Civil War. Hobbes was eager to have this last published, but the King would not give permission – it would stir up too much trouble. He was writing to the last, finishing his translation of Homer before finally leaving London in 1675, with a typical *boutade*: 'Why did I write it? Because I had nothing else to do. Why publish it? Because I thought it might take off my adversaries from showing their folly upon my more serious writings, and set them upon my verses to show their wisdom.' In his final retirement at Chatsworth and Hardwick – he moved with the household between the two – at ninety he wrote a last piece, 'Decameron Physiologicum', dialogues on physical questions, with yet another kick at Wallis' doctrine of gravitation and an obstinate adherence to an earlier demonstration in geometry.

In mid-October 1679, in his ninety-second year, he suffered a stroke and, when told that his state was incurable, said with typical humour: 'I shall be glad then to find a hole to creep out of the world at.' When the family was moving from Chatsworth to Hardwick he would not remain behind; laid on a feather bed they took him in their coach across the Derbyshire hills he had celebrated, to die in Bess of Hardwick's splendid house, where he had been much at home and where his memory lingers. All his life he had been taken care of by that famous family, a friend of three generations; on his side, too, he added to their fame, besides providing lively interest, instruction and amusement. He died on 4 December, and was buried in the little parish church of Ault Hucknall just outside the palings of the park. A black marble stone was placed above him, with a simple inscription. On this prospect, too, he had his joke: 'This is the true Philosopher's Stone.'

Everything shows that he was not the morose philosopher, the gruff old bear of popular legend – he would not have survived three generations in an aristocratic family if he had been, and we have seen what a mass of friends he had, all the way from his old schoolmaster at Malmesbury to the Merry Monarch. Aubrey bears witness to his essential kindliness: 'his goodness of nature and willingness to instruct anyone that was willing to be informed and modestly desired it ... I am a witness of as to my own part and also to others.' The provocations to his temper were all intellectual, for those were the matters he cared most about; then he could be sharp enough, for 'his work was attended with envy, which threw several aspersions and false reports on him'.

In practice he was given to charity – Aubrey was surprised at his leaving £1,000, considering what his charity had been, of which he gives several instances. Once, in the Strand, Hobbes confessed that it gave him pain to see the miserable condition of an infirm old man asking alms and – characteristically – that it eased his own pain to give him some relief, and this without any command of Christ. The rationalist hated cruelty in all its forms and often inveighed against Old Testament savagery, putting thousands to the sword by 'God's' command. He had taken care of his own family, providing for the education of his nephews and leaving them his money; he made his amanuensis – the Devonshires' baker, who wrote a delicate hand – his executor, giving him a pension.

Aubrey is more than usually informative as to the great man's habits, sharply observant of his appearance and personality. 'He was even in his youth generally temperate, both as to wine and women ... He never was, nor could not endure to be, habitually a good fellow, i.e. to drink every day wine with company which, though not to drunkenness, spoils the brain ... He rose about seven, had his breakfast of bread and butter, and took his walk meditating till ten; then he did put down the minutes of his thoughts, which he penned in the afternoon. When a line came into his head, he would as he was walking take a rude memorandum of it, to preserve it in his memory till he came to his chamber.' (Had he got that habit from Bacon?) 'He was never idle; his thoughts were always working.' The only fault one finds in him is his unworthy addiction to tobacco – though even this was in moderation.

'He was a tall man, higher than I am about half a head – six foot high and something better, and went indifferently erect or, rather, considering his great age, very erect. His sight and wit continued to the last; he had a curious sharp sight, as he had a sharp wit ... He had a good eye and that of a hazel colour, which was full of life and spirit even to his last; when he was in discourse there shone a bright live coal within it. He had two kinds of looks: when he laughed, was witty and in a merry humour, one could scarce see his eyes; by and by, when he was serious and positive, he opened his eyes round.'

He was wise in seldom using physic. 'Tis not consistent with an harmonical soul to be a woman-hater' – but we learn nothing as to any sex-life. He saved his vital spirits for better things.

CHAPTER 2

Hobbes on the Civil War

I

Hobbes's second work of importance on political events and their causes, second only to his *Leviathan*, is his *Behemoth: the History of the Causes of the Civil Wars of England, and of the Counsels and Artifices by which they were carried on from 1640 to 1660*. The sub-title not only tells us what it is about but gives us Hobbes's independent view of it without any illusions. He clearly intended the second work as a parallel to the first, or rather as an application to the concrete history of the Puritan Revolution of the general principles and view of society enunciated in the first. This is what happens when sovereignty breaks down, firm government falters and is challenged, people forget their duty to obey: chaos and anarchy follow, civil conflict, war and destruction, many thousands of good men's lives lost. For what? And why? And how?

The very titles, in their seventeenth-century fashion, suggested the parallel. Leviathan was the largest of sea-monsters. 'There go the ships, and there is that leviathan,' say the Psalms. And Milton:

> There Leviathan
> Hugest of living creatures, on the deep
> Stretched like a promontory sleeps or swims,

And seems a moving land, and at his gills
Draws in, and at his trunk spouts out a sea.

On the other hand, Milton describes Behemoth as 'biggest born of earth'; and the Book of Job, 'Behold now behemoth, which I made with thee; he eateth grass as an ox.'

Hobbes was able to publish *Leviathan* amid the turmoil, and in the freer air, of 1651. He wrote *Behemoth* when the honeymoon of the Restoration was over; about 1667-8, amid the disillusionments and defeats of the Dutch war, the plague of 1665 and the fire of London, and when Clarendon – the architect of the Restoration – was driven into exile in 1667. So the tone and temper are no more honeyed than that of *Leviathan*; actually sharper and more cynical – perhaps a better word would be more realist – because dealing with facts and events, men's follies and hypocrisies, the unexpected twists and turns, of two decades of the Puritan Revolution.

He was so scathing about it all that, though he submitted it to friendly Charles II (who would agree with most of it), the king would not take the risk of allowing it to appear. Too raw and near the bone, such a showing up of people's idiocies, when many of the actors were still about the place, still at it hammer and tongs, though the Restoration had prevented a further conflict. *Behemoth* received surreptitious publication a decade later in 1679; and a fuller edition amid the hysteria of the Popish Plot, Titus Oates and the execution of Popish lords, the envenomed party-conflict of Whig and Tory for power, which carried on in politics the struggle for power between Parliament and King, Puritans and Royalists, which had led to civil war.

Apparently the best manuscript of Hobbes's work lay silted up, ironically enough, in Laud's old college of St John's at Oxford.

Behemoth, then, illustrates and brings home the necessity of the principles of *Leviathan*: authoritarian rule,

simple and direct; strong government; law is what the
sovereign commands; it is the subject's duty to obey, not
challenge government – or anarchy ensues, as it had done.
In this book Hobbes holds up the appalling example, as a
mirror to concrete realities. Hence the bias of the book,
written from this point of view – how the monarchy broke
down. Hobbes really thought because it was too weak and
confused, and was weakened by half-Parliamentarian
Royalists like Clarendon. An imperceptive reader might
think that *Behemoth* was a Royalist tract, it would seem to
work out to that. But it is not: it is simply anti-revolutio-
nary – this was why he hated the Puritans. He had no use
for religious beliefs on one side or the other – he regarded
them as a chief cause everywhere of civil dissension. He is
no more a sympathiser with Archbishop Laud than with
Hugh Peters or Henry Marten.

The plebeian mind calls a spade a spade; he has no more
respect for kings than anybody else, except in so far as they
fulfil their purpose and rule firmly. (Charles I was
incapable of that; Cromwell ruled much more absolutely
and capably.) It may surprise the reader that Hobbes
wrote: 'God made kings for the people, and not people for
kings.' There was an equalism in Hobbes's mind, if not
egalitarianism – none of the sacramentalism of the true
Royalist: this was what was so shocking to Clarendon and
the bishops. Nothing was sacred to this lower-class man of
genius, who saw through everything, particularly anything
in the nature of humbug. Actually the title 'Behemoth'
seems to have run in his mind as early as his controversy
with Bishop Bramhall after *Leviathan*.

Hobbes realised that the war was the result of a conflict
for power and, in his down-to-earth way, that 'very few of
the common people cared much for either of the causes, but
would have taken any side for pay or plunder'. If the King
had only had the money for his army, he would have won.
This was very modern of Hobbes, no Victorian respect for

religious pretensions or pretences. He might almost be a pre-Marxist, or a precursor of Pareto, in regarding the religious disputes as an ideological smoke-screen for the conflict for power, the contemporary form which people's 'thinking' took. Hobbes was modern again in realising the importance of propaganda, and that the pulpit was the chief instrument of propaganda – preaching a Puritan weapon.

So he does attach importance to what was preached – preaching up rebellion: the Puritans had been engaged in propaganda against the establishment for three generations. The Civil War was the upshot. Hobbes didn't care tuppence for the supposedly religious content of what they preached – he thought that largely the nonsense it was; what the Presbyterians wanted was to take the place of the established church. 'Presbyterians are everywhere the same: they would fain be absolute governors of all they converse with; and have nothing to plead for it but that, where they reign, it is God that reigns, and nowhere else.'

He had no difficulty in recognising at the time the two main divisions that emerged with the Puritan Revolution, Presbyterians and Independents (i.e. Congregationalists), where modern academics have argued themselves into a state where they can't recognise a Puritan when they see one, or which sect is which. 'I do not believe that the Independents were worse than the Presbyterians: both the one and the other were resolved to destroy whatsoever should stand in the way to their ambition', i.e. to power.

The sects arose from people being allowed to interpret Scripture according to their own sweet will. 'After the Bible was translated into English every man – nay, every boy and wench – that could read English thought they spoke with God Almighty and understood what he said.' Hobbes describes the result. 'Some of them, because they would have all congregations free and independent, were called Independents. Others that held baptism to infants to be ineffectual were called therefore Anabaptists. Others that held that Christ's kingdom was at this time to begin upon the earth were called Fifth Monarchy men; besides divers other sects, as Quakers, Adamites, etc., whose names and peculiar doctrines I do not well remember.' He thought them all fools.

In accordance with the principles of the *Leviathan*, he would not have minded if they kept their folly to themselves; but they intermeddled with matters of state, wanted to impose their views on others beside themselves, were instruments of propaganda for more serious purposes, the contenders for power. Hobbes diagnosed that it was not 'their art' – i.e. their religion, that was so effective as that they had the concurrence of a great many of the gentry, 'that did no less desire a popular government in the civil state than these ministers did in the church'. This foreshadows modern views as to the origin of the war. 'In the beginning of the late war the power of the Presbyterians was so very great that, not only the citizens of London were almost all of them at their devotion, but also the greatest part of all other cities and market towns of England.' One wonders therefore how the King's cause was sustained; Hobbes tells us that Parliament did not think that he could raise an army. This is an example of the kind of miscalculation that brings wars about (the Germans did not think that Britain would fight in 1914 and 1939; or the Southern States in America that the North could fight in 1861).

It would probably have been better if Charles I had not raised an army, but waited in patience for the divisions among his opponents to develop. Clarendon said pleasantly that it would have been nice to leave the Presbyterians and Independents 'alone a while to convert one another, till they do both mend'.

The attack on the Church – which had brought Clarendon over to the King's side – went along with the challenge to government, 'to make them in love with democracy by their harangues in the Parliament and by their discourses in the country, continually extolling liberty and inveighing against tyranny, leaving the people to collect of themselves that this tyranny was the present government of the state.' Actually it was nothing of the kind: what we can say of the personal government of Charles I was that it was unrepresentative, inefficient and incapable of enforcing its wishes against the embattled stand of the gentry. Some of its aims were more enlightened than they – poor Archbishop Laud tried to protect the poor against their selfishness; one of these gentlemen, after a rating from him in Star Chamber, complained that he had been almost choked 'by a pair of lawn-sleeves.' The Archbishop was not a gentleman born; they saw to it that Star Chamber was abolished. No protection for the poor after the Restoration.

Hobbes diagnosed that 'though it be not likely that all of them did it out of malice, but many of them out of error, yet certainly the chief leaders were ambitious ministers and ambitious gentlemen: the ministers envying the authority of the bishops, and the gentlemen envying the Privy Council.' As for the ministers, Hobbes was as contemptuous as Milton came to be, after his disillusionment with them. Hobbes had never expected any better and describes their manner: 'they so framed their countenance and gesture at their entrance into the pulpit, and their pronunciation both in their prayer and sermon, and used the Scripture phrase – whether understood by the people or not, as that no tragedian in the world could have acted the part of a right godly man than these did.' To a civilised person, such as Charles I or Laud, it must have been insufferable. The Anglican clergy, adhering to the forms of the Prayer Book, were of course 'dumb dogs'; while the credulous people could not 'doubt that the vehemence of their voice – for the same words with the usual pronunciation had been of little force – and forcedness of their gesture and looks, could arise from anything else but zeal to the service of God'.

'Zeal' was for ever on their lips; after the collapse of their Revolution it became a favourite Nonconformist word. 'Hudibras' Butler pinpoints its utility:

> For Zeal is only proper to embroil,
> To overturn, disorder, and to spoil,
> But has no temper, judgment, nor discretion
> To manage things of consequence in reason;
> But Root and Branch,[1] at random, to demolish
> Unsight, unseen; and cross or pile abolish.

The demolition wrought by the Civil War was very considerable, which persons of no taste or artistic appreciation overlook: palaces like Basing House, Nonsuch or Holdenby were wrecked or fell into ruin; castles ruined or slighted all over the country; country houses burned; cathedrals, churches, chapels rifled of their treasures, stained glass, sculpture, woodwork destroyed; choirs dispersed, the glory of their music suspended, scattered, the tradition broken; the King's and nobles' such as Buckingham's collections of pictures and works of art sold abroad. Hobbes, no aesthete, did not consider these – the losses we chiefly regret.[2]

'You may reckon this among their artifices to make the people believe they were oppressed by the King, or perhaps by the bishops, or both'; while 'democratical gentlemen received them into their counsels for the design of changing the government from monarchical to popular, which they called liberty.' Another factor was that 'men of ancient wealth and nobility are not apt to brook that poor scholars should – as they must when they are made bishops – be

[1] This refers to the campaign for the abolition of episcopacy 'root and branch', afterwards enacted by Parliament.
[2] Cf. my *Reflections on the Puritan Revolution*.

their fellows'. This resentment entered into the hatred of Laud, who was not a gentleman by birth; Bishop Juxon, in spite of being Lord Treasurer, was not unpopular, because he was a gentleman, who rode to hounds. All the same lay nobles were jealous of clerics holding office, though the motive of the King's appointment of them was that their hands were clean; by the same token, Parliamentarians like Lord Saye and Sele were on edge to get the job of Lord Treasurer for its profits: as he did, and made a fortune out of it. Similarly all down the scale. Professor Mark Curtis has shown us that there was a surplus of university graduates, more than there were jobs for, and hence considerable black-coated clerical unemployment. Sheer envy at every level, up and down the scale, must not be discounted as a motive-force in making the revolution, as at other times in history.

Hobbes held no cynical view of the Anglican clergy: 'so much as they show of it in their life and conversation is for the most part very good, and of very good example.' This is a far more generous judgment than the scathing denunciations, of which we have all too much evidence, from Puritans who wanted to get them out of their livings and take their places. Hobbes had no prejudice in favour of Archbishop Laud; in fact, he described his upholding free-will against the Calvinist nonsense of predestination, rather harshly: 'His squabblings in the university about free-will; and his standing upon punctilios concerning the service book and its rubrics was not, in my opinion, an argument of his sufficiency in affairs of state.' Laud had to bear a shocking burden of vilification from nasty-minded Puritans: Hobbes dismissed them rightly as lies. They put it about that Laud was at heart a Papist – when no one stood more firmly for the Anglican position: in actual fact he converted a number of Catholics.

Laud was in a dangerous post, for at Court he was sabotaged by the Queen, a French Catholic, a light-headed

woman and a great liability to the King. In a madly
Protestant country she constantly proselytised for Catholicism, and had some success with silly women like
Buckingham's mother. She had priests and Capuchin friars
around her at Somerset House; 'also the resort of English
Catholics to the Queen's chapel gave them colour to blame
the Queen herself, not only for that but also for all the
favours that had been shown to the Catholics.' Laud wished
to hold the balance fairly, and to discourage Catholicism as
well as Puritanism; the balance was upset – and he was
unfairly blamed for it, even accused of conniving at it. His
execution in 1645, after some years in the Tower when he
might have been forgotten, was 'for nothing but to please
the Scots, for the general article of going about to subvert
the fundamental laws of the land was no accusation, but
only foul words'. Like Strafford, he was condemned to
death by attainder, i.e. murder by Act of Parliament.

Hobbes by no means abates his animus against the
universities for stirring up strife – the regular method of
proceeding by disputation inculcated disputatiousness, and
partly accounts for the nasty nature of religious controversy from Elizabeth I's reign onwards. 'Such curious
questions in divinity are first started in the universities,
and so are all those politic questions concerning the rights
of civil and ecclesiastical government. And there they are
furnished with arguments for liberty out of the works of
Aristotle, Plato, Cicero, Seneca, and out of the histories of
Rome and Greece, for their disputation against the
necessary power of their sovereigns.' Hobbes thought it
more important to obey the laws, 'to injure no man, to be in
charity with all men, to cherish the poor and the sick, and
to live soberly and free from scandal'. These were his
positive principles, and he lived in accord with them. He
deplored mixing up religion with 'points of natural
philosophy, as freedom of will, incorporeal substance,
everlasting nows, ubiquities, hypostases, which the people

understand not, nor will ever care for'.

He did not think that any of these controversies were 'necessary to salvation'. As for the Presbyterians, 'to believe in Christ is nothing with them, unless you believe as they do. Charity is nothing with them, unless it be charity and liberality to them and partaking with them in faction. The seditious doctrine of the Presbyterians has been struck so hard in the people's heads and memories – I cannot say into their hearts, for they understand nothing in it but that they may lawfully rebel – that I fear the commonwealth will never be cured.'

People thought that Hobbes's strictures on the universities and their teaching were unjustified, or perhaps exaggerated. But, he pointed out, a great number of Parliament men had had their training at the universities and imbibed their principles there. This was why Laud was so much concerned to reverse the trend. And we have already noticed how many of the extremists came from Hobbes's own university of Oxford, while Cambridge was the hot-bed of Puritanism. It may well be in some reaction against Hobbes that Oxford, for the next century, inculcated the doctrine of passive obedience. Nor are these things irrelevant today: Labour governments that have promulgated the brave new social order in Britain have been dominated by Oxford men, while the economists who have unloosened the nation's economy by their theorising have mostly come from Cambridge.

Let us turn to the delights of politics and the events of the rebellion those people preached, which led to Civil War.

II

Rebellion was announced by the killing of the King's chief minister, Strafford, 'whom they thought most able to prevent or oppose their further designs against the King'. They feared him for his ability and hated him as an apostate from the Parliamentarian party. It was untrue that he advised the King to use the army in Ireland against Parliament in England – though Vane perjured himself to say so; every member of the Council who heard it understood that Strafford referred to Scotland, then in rebellion. He was killed by act of attainder, i.e. by the will of the House of Commons – 'Stone dead hath no fellow' – while the Lords were overawed by the organised mob brought down to Westminster. Charles I gave way thinking to appease the opposition: he acknowledged it afterwards as his greatest mistake. Appeasement of the unappeasable is always a mistake.

Another error was the attempt, however well meant, to introduce a better order of church-service in Scotland. Archbishop Laud had been shocked, as well he might be, by the iconoclasm of the Reformation in Scotland. That in England had been bad enough, but it had at least spared the cathedrals: in Scotland they were largely ruined, like the most magnificent of them, St Andrew's – 'where the Scottish ministers first learned to play the fool', said Hobbes roundly. The Scots began the rebellion; Parliament connived at it, 'and put to the King's account the £300,000 given to the Scots, without which they would not have invaded England'. Hobbes was quite clear that, if it had not been for the intervention of the Scots, the King would have won the Civil War. At the end, they sold him to Parliament for another £200,000. What the impoverished Scots were really out for was money and loot.[3] We must remember this as an item that helps to account for the dislike of the Scots in England for the next century, especially with Tories like Swift and Dr Johnson.

Hobbes did not hesitate to say what shocked the conventional. He estimated that something like 100,000

---

[3] Cf. their destruction of the nave of Carlisle cathedral, and all the interior woodwork of Durham cathedral.

were killed in the war, in England, Scotland and Ireland. Would it not have been better, he asked, to have lined up the thousand preachers who preached sedition before they had done their work? 'It had been, I confess, a great massacre; but the killing of 100,000 is a greater.' It recalls Hitler's remedy for the challenge to British rule in India: line up a thousand of the leading agitators, and that would do the job. (Has the state of India been much better for the end of British rule – with hundreds of thousands of sectarian religious killings, four wars – three with Pakistan and one with China, and the open sore of India's unjust hold on Kashmir?) Hobbes has other reminders of Hitler or Stalin – both men of the people, who knew what the masses are. Hobbes says that it is much easier to gull the multitude than to gull one person. The epigraph to *Mein Kampf*, removed only just before Hitler's attainment of power, said: 'The German people have no idea how it has to be gulled in order to be led.'

Of course the people never understood the issue: 'the common people, whose hands were to decide the controversy, understood not the reasons of either party.' And, of course, they were taken advantage of. It was natural enough that the commercial classes of the cities should be of the rebel party, complaining of grievances, by which they meant taxes – compare the rumpus raised by John Hampden against a minimal charge of Ship Money. To the consideration that these employers at least set the poor to work, Hobbes replied – indeed, 'by making poor people sell their labour to them at their own prices'. This was Marx's argument about surplus-value. Hobbes said that the poor might get a better living in Bridewell, i.e. as unemployed. And as the people are first in the field, 'so also are they, for the most part, the first to repent, deceived by them that command their strength'. Hence the Clubmen, peasants and farmers rising to fend off both sides from depredations upon them.

2. Hobbes on the Civil War

Hobbes held that the position of Charles I was weakened by the proponents of mixed monarchy, i.e. a compromise with Parliament. He attacks the moderates – recognisably among them Clarendon, though not by name – 'whose pens the King most used in these controversies ... as having been members of this Parliament, and had declaimed against Ship Money and other extra-Parliamentary taxes as much as any; but who, when they saw the Parliament grow higher in their demands than they thought they would have done, went over to the King's party.' This was correct: Clarendon and his friends were in step with every move against the King's personal government and against Strafford, right up to the attack on the Church, when they realised at last that the Puritans meant no less than revolution.

Hobbes held that force was more forceful than 'all the arguments of law and force of argument', and if the King had stood firm people would have rallied to his side. But Charles wobbled between one course of action and another – as Clarendon said in his *History*; either one course or the other would have been better for him, it is not for us to say which, though Hobbes had no doubt. Certainly some of his advisers were fatal: the stupid Duke of Hamilton, who was the King's chief Scottish adviser, assured him that the Scots would not invade, and the King believed him. This was a crucial error. On the other hand, Parliament believed that the King would never be able to raise an army. One sees how people stumble into war through their misestimation of the other side.

The last section of Hobbes's book is therefore a salutary, and congenial, catalogue of the mistakes and follies committed on both sides.

There were also the chances and accidents of war. By 1643, Hobbes thought, Parliament had the stronger army, and 'if the Earl of Essex had immediately followed the King to Oxford, not yet well fortified, he might in all likelihood have taken it'. Conversely, the forces of the Earl of Newcastle were so strong in the North that, 'most men thought', if he had then marched southward and joined his forces with the King's, 'most of the members of Parliament would have fled out of England.' The Scottish army of 21,000 altered the balance – Hobbes describes it as 'hiring' them to invade England, and 'to compliment them in the meantime made a covenant ... and demolished crosses and church windows, such as had in them any images of the saints, throughout all England'. The chairman of the committee to direct the destruction was the Puritan Sir Robert Harley. Before his operations Henry VII's Chapel at Westminster had stained glass like that at King's College Chapel, Cambridge, by the same makers. Think of the loss! We have an example of the kind of thing that went on all over England from the detailed Journal of the miscreant Dowsing, who operated in Suffolk, Cambridgeshire and the Cambridge colleges.[4] It is a pity that the works of men's hands, their crafts and arts, should suffer for the nonsense they 'think'.

The King was curiously sanguine, over-optimistic; but, I suppose, 'Pour agir il faut espérer'. Hobbes was no actor in men's fooleries: he observed them. 'Why did the King trust himself with the Scots? They were the first that rebelled. They were Presbyterians; besides, they were indigent, and consequently might be suspected they would sell him to his enemies for money.' Hobbes's view of Cromwell was a cynical one, unjustly so: he held the Royalist view that Cromwell was scheming for power from the first, whereas he was an opportunist, a watchful politician, 'always applying himself to the faction that was strongest', in general poised to make the most of events, watchful till the moment for decision came.

Hobbes would not believe that Cromwell knew nothing

---

[4] For details see my *Reflections on the Puritan Revolution*.

about Cornet Joyce's action in flushing the King from Holdenby, to get him in the Army's power and out of Parliament's. In the developing conflict between Army and Parliament, 'the restoring of the King was but a reserve against the Parliament – which being in his pocket, he had no more need of the King, who was now an impediment to him'. Hobbes considered that the Scotch were displeased by the Army's enforcing the vote of no further addresses to the King, 'partly because their brethren the Presbyterians had lost a great deal of their power in England'. He did not think that Cromwell thought then to be king, 'but only by well serving the strongest party, which was always his main polity, to proceed as far as that and fortune would carry him'. Cromwell once said that no man went farther than he who knew not whither he was going – like Hitler who said that he went forward with the certainty of a somnambulist. When events turned out favourably Cromwell cited, 'Look at circumstantials! they hang so together', i.e. the action is justified merely by its success. The revolutionaries were uplifted by their early run of success, and regarded it as registering the approval of Providence. Then what when Providence turned against them in 1660, and the regicides found themselves on the gibbet?

Hobbes sums up to the execution of the King, with angry eloquence – 'the kingdom turned into a democracy, or rather an oligarchy; for presently they made an act that none of those members who were secluded for opposing the vote of no addresses should ever be re-admitted.' Parliament was down to a small Rump. He catalogues the crimes or follies of the Long Parliament to that date. 'What greater crimes than blaspheming and killing God's anointed: which was done by the hands of the Independents, but by the folly and first treason of the Presbyterians who betrayed and sold him to his murderers? Nor was it a little folly in the Lords not to see that by the taking away of the King's power they lost withal their own privileges. And for those men that had skill in the laws it was no great sign of understanding not to perceive that the laws of the land were made by the King, to oblige his subjects to peace and justice. And lastly and generally, all men are fools which pull down anything before they have set up something better in its place.' But of course they were ordinary humans, to whom the breakdown of authority gave opportunity to exhibit every variety of foolery – Hobbes saw it all as such. He might have said, with a disillusioned Liberal of our time, 'the longer I live the more I see that things really are as silly as they seem'.

Behemoth, like some others of Hobbes's works, is written in dialogue form. Liberty? What does it mean to the people? – 'Nothing but leave to do what they list.' What did the Commonwealth mean by 'the fundamental laws of the nation'? – 'Nothing but to abuse the people. For the only fundamental law in every commonwealth is to obey the laws, which he shall make to whom the people have given the supreme power. How likely then are they to uphold the fundamental laws that had murdered him who was by themselves so often acknowledged for their lawful sovereign?' Hobbes described the Rump, accurately, as an oligarchy: 'in the authority of few they thought the fewer the better, both in respect of their shares and also of a nearer approach in every one of them to the dignity of king.'

They levied far heavier taxes than the King had done and allowed their soldiers free quarter on people, 'which if the King had done, they would have said had been done against the liberty and property of the subject.' 'What silly things are the common sort of people to be cozened as they were so grossly?' – 'But what sort of people are not of the common sort? The craftiest knaves of all the Rump were no wiser than the rest whom they cozened.' And 'how have those ministers performed their office? – A great part of them, namely, the Presbyterian ministers throughout the whole war instigated the people against the King; so did also

Independents and other fanatic ministers.' 'To what end? –
To the end that the state becoming popular the Church
might be so too, and governed by an Assembly; and by
consequence they might govern and thereby satisfy not
only their covetous humour with riches, but also their
malice with power to undo all men that admired not their
wisdom.'

Hobbes hated the guts of the religious sects; of course he
detested them as fomenters of civil dissension, but in this
way he could express indirectly, what would otherwise
have been dangerous, his disbelief in religion as such.

The civil war in Ireland exhibited as much dissension
and folly, and – Ireland being a more backward, regressive
society – there it was even more barbarous and savage. An
overwhelming majority existed against Parliament, in the
coalition between the confederate Royalists, Protestant
and Catholic, with the Catholic resistance under the
leadership of an Italian Nuncio. This last was interested
only in the extension of Papal authority, and thus lost the
game to the small minority of Puritans, who had more
energy and sense. The unwieldy coalition, riven by disputes
about command, was at last defeated by a mere sally out of
Dublin, led by one Jones. Thereupon arrived Cromwell,
'who with extraordinary diligence and horrid executions,
in less than a twelve-month that he stayed there, subdued
in a manner the whole nation.' Nations, as well as
individuals, get what they deserve for their follies.

Scotland was no better. Hobbes regarded the execution of
gallant Montrose, by the Covenanters of Edinburgh as
'more spiteful usage than revenge required'. When, after
Charles I's execution, they called Charles II to Scotland,
the Presbyterians 'would not suffer either the King, or any
royalist, to have command in the army'. Thus they depleted
their forces and refused to avail themselves of many
experienced officers. They got their come-uppance from
Cromwell at Dunbar, where the Scots – urged on by their

divines – threw away an impregnable position. 'Thus the folly of the Scottish commanders brought all their odds to an even lay between two small and equal parties; wherein fortune gave the victory to the English, who were not many more in number than those that were killed and taken prisoners of the Scots. And the Church [i.e. the Kirk] lost their cannon, bag and baggage, with 10,000 arms and almost their whole army.' Thus 'the Scotch ecclesiastics began to know themselves better, and resolved in their new army, which they meant to raise, to admit some of the Royalists into command'. Too late: Scotland lay open to Cromwell, while his victories in Ireland and Scotland together advanced his power in England.

Hobbes's account of the Rump's Dutch war is in similar terms of men's self-interest, greed and folly. 'The Rump showed now as little desire of agreement as the Dutch did … [both] standing upon terms never likely to be granted.' 'The true quarrel, on the English part, was that their proffered friendship was scorned; on the Dutch part was the greediness to engross all traffic, and a false estimate of our and their own strength.' Once more Hobbes hits on this crucial factor in the causation of war – the miscalculation of the opposite side by one, or both, of the opponents.

By this time the Rump of a Parliament 'had already lost the hearts of the generality of the people, and had nothing to trust to but the Army, which was not in their power but Cromwell's: who never failed, when there was occasion, to put them upon all exploits that might make them odious to the people.' When his 'patience was exhausted' Cromwell sent Parliament packing; 'and for this action he was more applauded by the people than for any of his victories in the war, and the Parliament men as much scorned and derided.' Such are the ironies of history, when we reflect what a cult the name of Parliament commanded in 1640.

It is significant that Hobbes lets off Cromwell lightly, and hardly condemns him at all. 'Yes, certainly, he had as good a title as the Long Parliament. But the Long Parliament did represent the people; and it seems to me that the sovereign power is essentially annexed to the representative of the people.' Evidently – no sacramentalism, no nonsense about the divine right of kings: it is never even mentioned by Hobbes: we see peeping out, rather, what we might call his popular equalism. The point here is answered with a qualification: 'nor was the Lower House of Parliament the representative of the whole nation, but of the commons only.'

'Did Cromwell come in upon the only title of *salus populi*?' (i.e. the well-being of the people). – 'This is a title that very few men understand. His way was to get the supreme power conferred upon him by Parliament. Therefore he called a Parliament and gave it the supreme power, to the end that they should give it to him again. Was not this witty?' (Charles II must have appreciated this sally.)

Hobbes hardly goes into the events of Cromwell's autocratic rule. No doubt it raised a problem for him; for, though Clarendon was incorrect in his repeated charges that Hobbes was making up to Cromwell in the *Leviathan*, it was in keeping with its principles that people should submit to a *de facto* ruler once it was clear that he possessed the power. We may well think that Hobbes admired the ablest politician-cum-soldier who had come out on top and given the country firm rule – even Clarendon confessed a reluctant admiration for Cromwell's 'great heart'. Hobbes would have drawn the line at the man's hysterical religiosity, of course, which had driven him into rebellion and all that followed.

Hobbes describes briefly and contemptuously the dissensions, the chops and changes, that followed upon Cromwell's death: the brief episode of his undistinguished son, the inveterate quarrel between the army and the politicians, the return of a rump of the Rump, the fatuous arguments of the idealogues and doctrinaires, the Harringtons, Nevilles, Miltons. On Milton Hobbes has his own word in *Behemoth*, condemning both Salmasius' attack on the King's execution and Milton's defence of it. 'They are very good Latin both, and hardly to be judged which is better; and both very ill reasoning, hardly to be judged which is worse. Like two declamations, *pro* and *con*, made for exercise only in a rhetoric school by one and the same man. So like is a Presbyterian to an Independent.' Milton, for his part, could not but admire Hobbes's parts, while deploring his principles.

At the end Hobbes spotlights the decisive money-power of the City of London. The army could not retain power without it, and the City was opposed to the heavy burden of a large army, upon which Cromwell's rule had rested. But the City was also opposed to the Rump, 'and keen upon a free Parliament'. Everybody – except the idealogues – knew what that would bring about: Clarendon was in the end right, only government based on the old model could give permanence. Hobbes censured the City: 'but for the City the Parliament never could have made the war, nor the Rump ever have murdered the King.'

Hobbes sums up, clearly and decisively, the whole course of the Puritan Revolution in his own terms. 'First, from 1640 to 1649, when the King was murdered, the sovereignty was disputed between King Charles I and the Presbyterian Parliament. Secondly, from 1649 to 1653, the power was in that part of the Parliament which voted the trial of the King, and declared themselves, without King or House of Lords, to have the supreme authority of England and Ireland. For there were in the Long Parliament two factions, the Presbyterian and Independent: the former whereof sought only the subjection of the King, not his destruction directly: the latter sought directly his destruction. Thirdly, from 20 April to 4 July 1653, the supreme power was in the hands of a Council of State directed by Cromwell. Fourthly, from 4 July to 12 December of the same year it was in the hands of men called unto it by Cromwell, whom he termed men of fidelity and integrity, and made them a Parliament; which was called, in contempt of one of its members, Barebone's Parliament. Fifthly, from 12 December 1653 to 3 September 1658, it was in the hands of Oliver Cromwell, with the title of Protector. Sixthly, from 3 September 1658 to 25 April 1659, Richard Cromwell had it as successor to his father. Seventhly, from 25 April to 7 May of the same year, it was nowhere. Eighthly, from 7 May 1659 the Rump, which was turned out of doors in 1653, recovered it again, and shall lose it again to a committee of safety, and again recover it, and again lose it to the right owner.' The Restoration of Charles II is seen to be inevitable.

We observe that Hobbes's account of historical events is entirely in terms of power. He takes that for granted, rightly, for that is what politics are about. It is equally noticeable that his intellectual interest is mainly devoted to the follies, self-interest and dissensions of the religious sects – they had preached up the Puritan Revolution and then shown how incompetent they were to maintain it. Hobbes detested them, but what elicited most his personal scorn – were people's stupidity and credulity, the varieties of religious nonsense. Hobbes was not alone in this: some of the most brilliant intellects of the time were largely in agreement – Bacon, Lord Herbert of Cherbury, Selden, Samuel Butler, Halifax, Locke. Hobbes's detestation of nonsense had a vehemence which led on to Swift and Voltaire. Everything Hobbes wrote produced controversy, and nobody relished what he wrote about people or politics. Little did he care about that: he had no respect for other people's opinions; confidence in his own genius carried him forward to write for himself and for posterity.

Today we can appreciate how modern his outlook was, in keeping with the appalling events of our own time. It is

CHAPTER 3

Henry Marten: Republican and Regicide

I

I cannot conceal from myself that I am more sympathetic to
Henry Marten than I should have expected. After all he
was a Parliamentarian, an uncompromising enemy of the
King throughout the Civil War, a republican and
(unforgivably) a regicide. Perhaps it is that, in spite of this
catalogue of offences, he was no Puritan; as John Aubrey
said of him, 'he was as far from a Puritan as light from
darkness'. That is already something: he was no humbug.
One feels about him as Cobbett felt about the prime
advantage of visiting the United States – 'above all, no
Wilberforces. Think of that: no Wilberforces!' For what
there was to be said in his favour we shall see. He was, at
any rate, no believer – in that age when people were
knocking each other on the head for their ridiculous beliefs.

His was an arresting and vital personality – if an
abortive career – with an interesting background. It was
something to have been disapproved of alike by Charles I
and Oliver Cromwell. Aubrey tells us that 'Henry was in
Hyde Park one time when his Majesty was there, going to
see a race. The King espied him and said aloud, "Let that
ugly rascal be gone out of the park, that whoremaster, or
else I will not see the sport." ' Aubrey dramatised the
incident in his usual manner, saying that Henry went away

patiently, but had his own revenge. 'That sarcasm raised the whole county of Berks against him', i.e. the King; for Marten bore great sway in Berkshire, through his money, his hospitality and perhaps other qualities. Some years later, when Oliver Cromwell sent the Rump Parliament packing and assumed the government as Protector, he charged, looking pointedly at Marten and his crony Sir Peter Wentworth, that they were 'whoremasters'. Cromwell and Charles I were in this respect alike – respectable.

One day Marten imparted to a fellow MP – it was Edward Hyde, to become the great Clarendon – that he did not think 'one man wise enough to govern us all'. This youthful sentiment, which *sounds* so wise, has been disproved by events in all revolutions. It was disproved by Cromwell himself, who took on the government and ruled with great ability, when the Parliamentary factions simply could not hold together. As again in our own time, when the Russian Revolution could hold on its course only by a succession of one-man rulers – Lenin, Stalin, Krushchev, Brezhnev. What *sounds* so plausible is frequently contradicted by facts in politics.

Whence did young Marten get his plausible political ideas, democratic, anti-monarchy, republican? Hobbes thought that seventeenth-century youth imbibed them from the classical authors, with their republican sympathies, whom they studied at the university. It is true that young people pick up silly ideas at the university – an occupational hazard which, I suppose, has to be undergone. And it is indeed noticeable how many of these republican doctrinaires were at Oxford – Marten himself, his friends Thomas Chaloner, Sir Peter Wentworth, Henry Neville, Sir Henry Vane, Ludlow, not to mention the more powerful, less doctrinaire, Ireton, Cromwell's son-in-law and right-hand man.

Marten had no reason for resentment from his paternal background. His father, Sir Henry Marten, made a fortune as a royal official; he was a self-made man, and he made a lot. The grandfather was a mere copyholder of £60 a year; his son became worth some £3,000 a year (multiply by any number of times for the inflationary 'values' of today). Sir Henry, a Wykehamist and New College man, made it out of the civil and canon law in which he had a wide practice. He rose to become a judge of the High Court of Admiralty and, as an ecclesiastical lawyer, a member of Archbishop Laud's High Court of Commission and Dean of Arches – a most unpromising background, one would have thought, for a son who was irreligious, a republican and a regicide.

Sir Henry wisely put his winnings into several estates in Berkshire, a splendid patrimony which his gifted son dissipated. Two of these, Longworth and Hinton Waldrist, neighbour each other along the pleasant escarpment that runs by Faringdon overlooking the upper Thames Valley. Sir Henry was buried in Longworth church, though his extravagant son did not provide him with a monument. The younger Henry lived principally at another estate, Becket, of which the rebuilt manor-house is now the officers' mess of the Royal Military College at Shrivenham. He occasionally spent a night – as indeed once did Oliver Cromwell – at exquisite Hinton Waldrist, where some parts of the Tudor house are embedded in the lovely Queen Anne and Regency house built by his successors.

Money, everything, ran through his hands. It was said that in his father's lifetime Henry was costing him £1,000 a year, the second son £500. A little horsewhipping would have been in order – except that nothing kept the younger Henry in order. To repair some of the damage, 'his father found out a rich wife for him, whom he married something unwillingly.' (This lady was the widowed sister of Lord Lovelace.) 'He was a great lover of pretty girls, to whom he was so liberal that he spent the greatest part of his estate. When he found out a married woman that he liked (and he had his emissaries, male and female, to look out), he would contrive such or such a good bargain, £20 or £30 per annum under-rent, to have her near him. He lived from his wife a long time. If I am not mistaken, she was sometime distempered by his unkindness to her.' He kept her at Longworth. What a fool this clever man was!

He quarrelled with his friend Sir William Platers over a woman. Sir William was 'a great admirer and lover of handsome women, and kept several. Henry Marten and he were great cronies, but one time (about 1644) there was some difference between them ... Marten invited him to a treat, where Sir William fell in love with one of his misses and slockst her away. Sir John Birkenhead inserted in his *Mercurius Aulicus* how the Saints fell out.' It must be admitted that Henry Marten never pretended to be a saint, unlike so many of them. Indeed he never pretended to anything: it was his prime disadvantage as a politician that he was totally without humbug (in which Cromwell was supreme). What Marten had was wit, and this made him a speaker much listened to in the Long Parliament – that and his perfectly clear convictions, where most people were confused and engaged in merely reacting to events, which is what most people's 'thinking' comes to. This gave him a lead, and he became the centre of the republican 'gang' – as it was called at the time – in Parliament, long before events caught up with his views and made them not only relevant but effective. Even his wit – rusty as that seventeenth-century weapon has mostly become to us – can still reach across the centuries as that of few others of the time.

Again and again Marten was beforehand with events and over important issues – the monarchy, the rôle of the Commons, the dispensability of the House of Lords, religious toleration, law reform, electoral and social reforms, particularly in regard to imprisonment for debt, a subject on which he was to have personal experience. He began his career of opposition to the Crown by refusing to

3. Henry Marten: Republican and Regicide

contribute to the expense of Charles I's Scottish war in 1639 (events were to make him anti-Scots later under Parliament, such is the irony of life and history). His refusal made him a hero in Berkshire, as John Hampden's unreasonable refusal to pay Ship Money made him a national hero. Marten was thereupon returned to both the Short and the Long Parliament in 1640, as knight of the shire for Berkshire.

Quite early in the struggle with the King Marten took up an extreme position. He was one of those most zealous against Strafford and anxious to bring him to the block by attainder instead of impeachment, i.e. taking his life by act of Parliament since no treason could be proved against him. Later, Marten was to revise his opinion on this procedure, which was simply 'judicial' murder, in favour of impeachment by due process in which a defendant could defend himself. (It was used again, indefensibly, against Laud.) Marten argued, too, that ordinances of Parliament were valid without royal assent: revolutionary as this was, it suited Parliament's book, pushing forward the Puritan Revolution. The excuse was that the King intended to levy war – and indeed he had been pushed into doing so. In the Declaration of his case in taking up arms, August 1642, the King condemned Marten for publicly proclaiming that 'our office is forfeitable, and that the happiness of the kingdom doth not depend on us, nor any of the regal branches of that stock'. Charles I regarded this rightly as treasonable, and excepted Marten from future pardon.

Meanwhile he was doing his bit in Berkshire, raising a regiment of horse on his own and subscribing £1,200 to the cause, which became the Good Old Cause to adherents and its nostalgic admirers today. Made Parliamentary governor of Reading, Marten showed that he was not of the stuff of which soldiers are made – he was a talker, *und sonst nichts*. On the approach of the King's army he somewhat hastily evacuated the position for Westminster, the real forum of his activities. From those depleted benches – one third of the members had withdrawn to the King – he was well able to urge on the war, oppose negotiations for peace, and criticise others for tardiness or inaction. The Earl of Essex, for example, lay inert at Windsor while the Royalists scored successes in the West and the North. Marten commented that it was 'summer in Devonshire, summer in Yorkshire, and only winter at Windsor'. This recalls, and probably repeats, Elizabeth I's celebrated reproof to Essex's father in Ireland.

Until his death 'King Pym' dominated the scene, prosecuting the war while holding the door open for negotiations – on Parliament's terms, of course. Marten urged the rejection of the King's reasonable offers and, when the House of Lords objected to Marten's seizure of the King's horses he said that he saw no reason why the King's horses should not be taken as well as his ships. The royal navy had been seduced from its allegiance by a member of the House of Lords, the Earl of Warwick: it was like Marten to make a quip that was as pointed as it was logical. No aesthete, with more taste for tarts than the arts, he was a member of the committee for destroying the works of art – 'superstitious images' – in the Queen's chapel at Somerset House. The Rubens altar-piece was thrown into the Thames. Of the splendid regalia in Westminster Abbey he said that 'there would be no further use of these toys and trifles'. This was before the execution of the King, when the proclamation of a republic made them superfluous, and these priceless medieval objects were broken up and destroyed.

In April 1643 Marten occasioned an awkward breach at Westminster by opening the Earl of Northumberland's letters to his wife. Clarendon says that 'this insolence was not disliked'; the inwardness of it was that Marten suspected information about negotiations with the King, to which his faction was opposed. At a conference between the

Houses in the Painted Chamber the arrogant Northumberland, standing by the fire, asked Marten for an explanation. On receiving a justification instead, the Earl struck the MP with a cane. At once swords were drawn and the privileges of the Commons cited. There was much ado to appease the fracas, which rejoiced the Royalists at Oxford, who got a full account into their paper, *Mercurius Aulicus*.

In August 1643 Marten was in more serious trouble for offending Parliamentary humbug itself. Parliament's position was that it was fighting for King *and* Parliament, that it was not fighting the King but his noxious advisers. This was mere politics, of course, but useful propaganda. A meddling minister – of whom there were far too many – one Saltmarsh, blew the gaff upon this in a pamphlet urging that the surest way to gain the people was to present the war as one against Popery and, as for the King, if he would not capitulate then to root him out and the royal line, and have someone else. (This ultimately was done, with the Glorious Revolution of 1688.) Parliament was affronted by such base interpretation of its acts. But Marten spoke up for the tactless minister, saying that it were better one family should be destroyed than many. Interrogated as to which family he meant, though it was obvious enough, he boldly answered, 'The King and his children.' This piece of candour greatly angered respectable members, who threw back at him his 'lewdness of life'; he was censured by the great Pym himself, expelled from Parliament and sent briefly to the Tower.

Once more *Mercurius Aulicus* had reason to crow – that 'Marten's punishment should be inflicted by them who had ever till now encouraged him in the crime, for indeed his language was but the sense of the House'. This was true enough; but the Royalists were of the opinion that 'there has grown some heartburning betwixt Marten and Pym about their shares in the public Faith-Money, Master

Marten conceiving Master Pym swept too much away for one single Member ... and that he [Marten] had spent more than he had gained since the beginning of this Parliament, but others had gotten many thousands by their Memberships'. This also was true, but it was tactless to say it. Pym was the leader of Parliament, living in state in the Earl of Derby's house, with his own private coach; when he died he was given the funeral of a prince.

Marten may have filled in time in the army during his expulsion from Parliament, for he is sometimes referred to as Colonel. At New Year 1646 he was readmitted and at once resumed his leadership of his 'gang', pressing for more extreme courses, opposing the Presbyterian grandees, opening the way for the Independents whose chief patron was Cromwell, and even holding out a hand towards the Levellers, whose leader was 'honest John' Lilburne. It is now thought that Marten had some part in formulating the second 'Agreement of the People'. The Lilburnes, however, were doing well out of a royalist's estate in the North, as that other Leveller, John Wildman, was to make a fortune out of forfeited royalist estates in the South. It should be made clear that Marten was not a Leveller, and made nothing out of other people's property; he spent only what was his own. It should also be emphasised that Cromwell's radicalism was merely religious; socially he was a conservative, as became a gentleman with his aristocratic connexions; politically, he would have preferred constitutional monarchy – events (and the instinct of self-preservation) drove him to take the King's life, not republican doctrinairism.

The statesmanlike Pym had purchased the Scotch alliance at the price of imposing the ridiculous Presbyterian Covenant upon England – and this won the war for Parliament. The English, however, were not having this nonsense riveted upon their necks – and Marten was an Englishman, if not exactly a 'good' one. He described the

70

Covenant as 'an almanach of last year', and expressed the opinion of most Englishmen about the Scotch imposition as a worse burden than the King's. 'A king is but one master, and therefore likely to sit lighter upon our shoulders than a whole kingdom ... and he may be sooner gotten off than they.' This also proved true.

Parliament's victory in the civil war provided no solution to the problem as to how the country was to be governed – there was more danger of social break-up, mutiny in the army, clubmen at large in the counties, famine and plague in some areas, idiotic sects proliferating, social agitation spreading – and what wonder when the governing class had been so foolish as to get divided in an internal struggle for power? At any moment the people would have voted the King back, after all their sufferings and deceptions. When he was confined at Holdenby House, and negotiations went backwards and forwards, the people flocked to him to be touched for the King's Evil by the sacrosanct hand of an anointed king – such are the people. Henry Marten said, with his shocking commonsense, that the Parliament's Great Seal might do as well, if there were an ordinance for it.

Marten grew suspicious of Cromwell's negotiations – for Oliver, like the politician he was, was usually capable of compromise. In September 1647 Marten moved a vote of No Addresses to the King, to be voted down. Once more he anticipated the way things would move. There was no real compromise with Charles I except on *his* terms; the Second Civil War brought that home. Nevertheless the Presbyterian leaders in Parliament continued negotiations, partly out of fear of their own Army. Marten withdrew to Berkshire to raise another regiment on his own, without the authority of Parliament, and no doubt for use against it if they were to restore the King. His authority, he claimed, was 'on behalf of the people of England, for the recovery of their freedom'. We see that he was susceptible of some humbug – democratic humbug – for the people would certainly have restored the King. Parliament sent forces to disperse Marten's adherents, who were moved up north to join Cromwell. Marten and Cromwell – unlikely partners – joined hands for a time in bringing the King to book.

Charles I was held responsible for the Second Civil War and for bringing in the Scots again, as Parliament had done five years before. The Army put through a purge of the Presbyterians who had been dominant in Parliament, upon which the motion of No Addresses to the King was at length passed and his 'trial' embarked upon. Marten was a foremost proponent of the shameful proceedings, became one of the King's 'judges' and signed the death-warrant. When someone inquired by what authority, it was Marten who suggested, 'In the name of the Commons in Parliament assembled, and all the good people of England.' This was a very different inflexion from the authoritarian Cromwell's, who said: 'To give votes to men that have no interest but the interest of breathing would be anarchy.' When, later, Cromwell was setting out to battle with the Scots and was cheered by the mob, he said to his companion that the same scum would cheer if they were on their way to the gallows. He *knew*. However, the emergency drew the democrat and the general together: years later Marten's servant deposed that at the signing of the death-warrant these two miscreants spattered each other's faces with the ink. Cromwell's hysterical temperament was liable to seek relief in horse-play at moments of tension; there is no such excuse for Marten, it was merely his way.

II

In the constitutional hiatus that supervened Henry Marten was prepared: he at least had a policy, events had caught up with his republicanism. In this area at least he was a real believer. He suggested the device and inscription for the new Great Seal: 'In the first year of freedom by God's blessing restored' – we may take it that 'by God's blessing' was for popular consumption and did not represent his beliefs. He had the delightful charge of taking down the King's arms from public places: 'Exit Tyrannus Regum ultimus', and so on. A small committee of the Rump Parliament placed him on the new Council of State, upon which we may watch his activities during the first year from the State Papers, if only as a sample.

He was placed on a number of the Council's important committees. In February one of two to prepare instructions for those to go to Scotland; to consider the precedence of ambassadors to the new Republic; with Cromwell to consider the forces necessary to subdue Ireland. In March: to consider alliances with foreign states and whether to continue them. For foreign relations it was necessary to appoint a secretary acquainted with foreign tongues. John Milton deserved well of the Republic for his defence of the King's execution. Marten was one of the committee to ask Mr Milton if he would undertake the job. Would a duck swim? It was just the kind of job the fanatical Puritan had been looking for, ambitious for public employment and acclaim. On acceptance Mr Milton was at once asked to make observations on the complications of interest among designers against the peace of the Commonwealth. With Marten's growing interest in foreign affairs he must have been brought into some contact with the upright little secretary. We have no information as to how the chaste Milton regarded the wicked Marten; but Milton became friendly with Marten's disreputable crony, Sir Peter Wentworth, who years later left a legacy of £100 to 'my worthy and very learned friend, Mr John Milton, who writ against Salmasius' – who had attacked the 'judicial' murder of the King.

In these enthusiastic months Marten served on

committees which dealt with matters great and small, most of some urgency in the state of affairs: for preserving timber for shipbuilding, for making saltpetre for gunpowder, to consider treaties and alliances, the funeral of Dr Dorislaus. How perilous was the situation of the infant Republic was brought home by the assassination of this envoy by royalists in Holland. Several times Marten was involved in examining the irrepressible Levellers brought before Parliament, in particular Lilburne whom Marten treated with marked sympathy. He had indeed had dealings with Lilburne before the King's execution and some part in moderating the demands put forward in the third draft of the 'Agreement of the People'; for, without being a Leveller, Marten seriously wished for reform of the electoral system. From one of Lilburne's imprisonments in the Tower Marten got him out: he had kindly impulses – except for kings.

In June we find him conferring with the Lord General, Cromwell, as to the quartering of soldiers in towns – a problem which had vexed Charles I in his early years and led to the Petition of Right. Marten was to consider the great feast ordered in celebration of victory in London, to report on the case of the former farmers of Customs and to the House of Commons on an immense mass of business accumulating. He was to confer also on such a small matter as the names of JPs for Cornwall. Here we see how small was the basis of support for the new régime in the country, for only two recognisable names turn up – and those of the smaller gentry, an Erisey and a Langdon, the rest unknowns.

In August Marten served on the committee for bringing money into the Treasury; in September for the pay of the Army, and drawing up a declaration to it of the danger of being misled into engagements against Parliament – here yawned the rift which ultimately engulfed the Republic and brought about the Restoration. That month the

Jack-in-the-box Lilburne popped up again, for Marten to deal with. In October, the committee to survey the timber in Windsor and Epping forests, to decide what was fit for shipping, what for sale – a prime necessity from all the burdens of the war, still continuing in Ireland and at sea, and of the Army upon which the régime depended. In November the garrison of Liverpool in need of repair was to be considered, in December measures to prepare for its strengthening.

Such was Marten's committee work alone on the Council of State in that first year of freedom by God's blessing restored. Besides this there was his regular attendance in Parliament, where he was the linch-pin of his Republican gang – and other activities, his pamphleteering, along with his well-publicised private pleasures. He was much in touch with the City of London, a favourite with commercial interests there, for which he had upon occasion made himself a spokesman. But it does not appear to be true, what has been said, that he was not an attentive Councillor of State, at least in this first year of revolution when it was bliss to be alive.

The enthusiastic Republican saw no point in a House of Lords – here again he was in opposition to the more traditional views of Cromwell. When the House of Lords was attacked as 'useless and dangerous', one of his jokes was that it was 'useless, but not dangerous'. Marten won; the House was abolished – collaborationist peers like Pembroke and Salisbury could sit in the Commons. We must not underrate Marten's genuine interest in reforms, particularly for relief of poor prisoners for debt – the one respect in which he had any success. His aims for law reform were aborted by the conservatism of the lawyers; in October 1650 he chaired the committee for law reform, to have its proposals once more emasculated – one sensible step only was taken: proceedings were to be in English, instead of the ludicrous lawyers' Norman-French which put their trade-union expertise at a premium. (This was restored at the Restoration.)

On religious issues Marten was up against the embattled prejudices of the Presbyterian majority in the Rump. He favoured toleration, which was anathema to them, and even proposed that this should include Catholics. This, of course, was shocking. Tithes for the support of the clergy were inextricably bound up with the whole system of landholding and agricultural operations in every parish. They were a great source of grievance, and Marten would have liked to end them. But this would have meant social revolution, added to the political, and Cromwell settled for the existing system. Before the end of his rule his brother-in-law Wilkins told him that the church in England could be run only by bishops – and at the Restoration Wilkins sensibly became one.

Puritan moral humbug must have been equally anathema to Marten – ludicrous, if it were not so barbarous. The opportunity for moral reform for which the Puritans had agitated for a couple of generations came with their victory in the Civil War. As early as December 1644 the Commons ordered a bill to be brought in to repress whoredom, adultery, incest, drunkenness and other pleasures. In 1650 they passed their monstrous act to punish adultery with death – the culmination of Puritan propaganda for decades, inspired by their Old Testament mania. James I, an intelligent king, had told the Commons, what any civilised person would have known, that the law of Moses was the law of Israel, 'only fit for that country, that people and time'. Archbishop Whitgift, another civilised man, held the humane view that the coming of Christ had abrogated the savagery of the Law of Moses.

This was not good enough for his Presbyterian opponent, Cartwright, or for the New England Saint, William Ames, the odious Prynne or most of the leading Puritans. They got their chance with the Puritan Republic, and in 1650 made adultery and fornication punishable with death – even so, in accordance with Old Testament savagery, punishment fell harder on the offending woman than the man. Naturally Marten opposed this wicked nonsense, in a speech conceived to turn the flank of its proponents. With his usual shocking commonsense, and his tongue in his cheek, he said, according to the sobersides Lord Keeper Whitelocke, that 'the severity of the punishment by this act, which was death, would cause these sins to be more frequently committed. Because people would be more cautious in committing them for fear of the punishment, and being undiscovered would be emboldened the more in the commitment of them.' That would seem to reduce the humbug to its proper level – though a modern protagonist of the Puritans, Christopher Hill, expounds the Act as aiming to preserve the purity of family life.

Marten was a humane and kindly man. He twice obtained Lilburne's release from imprisonment, and another time secured the payment of his arrears. He was instrumental in saving the life of Judge David Jenkins, an obstinate Royalist who would have been hanged if it were not for Marten. Aubrey has a story that Marten helped to save Davenant's life with a joke – 'in the House, when they were talking of sacrificing one, then said Henry that "in sacrifices they always offered pure and without blemish: now ye talk of making a sacrifice of an old rotten rascal".' (Davenant was much blemished by venereal disease: he had lost his nose.) The joke is very much in Marten's shameless manner; it seems more likely that he helped to mitigate the royalist poet's imprisonment.

There was much sympathy for Lilburne among the women. Three times a posse of them came down to the House to petition on his behalf. The Commons would not receive them, but at length sent out the answer that 'the matter was of an higher concernment than they understood; that the House gave an answer to their husbands, and therefore desired them to go home and look after their own business, and meddle with their house-wifery.' This was much after the Puritan mind, with its masculine prejudice in keeping with the barbarism of the Old Testament. It illuminates the ludicrous attitude of Milton as to the inferiority of women – so unlike the cultivated Court of Charles I. Something of the inflexion appears in the appalling persecution of old women as witches, which marked the Puritan triumph – there had been none under the civilised King and Archbishop. A few months after Charles I's execution Whitelocke notes that in Presbyterian Edinburgh five witches had been burnt alive, 'who had marks upon them which they had from the Devil'. That autumn he reported yet more women burned as witches in Scotland: two on 3 September, eleven next day, and some twenty-five before: a holocaust by these poisonous Puritan fanatics. No wonder Marten was anti-Scots, anti-clerical, anti-religious. In England the execution of the intriguing minister, Christopher Love, for plotting against the Commonwealth broke the back of the clerical opposition to the Rump. After that, Richard Baxter said, the ministers regarded the Commonwealth as tyranny – which it was, and they had asked for it.

Marten's jokes strike one as simple enough today; not many in that sour assembly, the Rump, can have had much sense of humour. Aubrey tells us that 'his speeches in the House were not long, but wondrous poignant [i.e. pointed], pertinent and witty. He was exceeding happy in apt [i.e. personal] instances. He alone has sometimes turned the whole House. Making an invective speech one time against old Sir Henry Vane, when he had done with him, he said, "But for young Sir Henry Vane" – and so sat him down. Several cried out, "What have you to say to young Sir Harry?" He rises up: "Why, if young Sir Harry lives to be old, he will be old Sir Harry." ' Perhaps that was enough. The young Vane, intellectually arrogant and conceited, as rich as he was vain, was disliked by everybody – except Milton, the apple of whose eye he was. (Everybody else was out of step, except those two.) Though a religious enthusiast of his own incomprehensible persuasion, Vane came to be distrusted even by Cromwell: 'O, Sir Harry Vane – God preserve me from Sir Harry Vane!' Naturally Marten detested him and managed to keep him off one of the Rump's Councils of State.

In 1650 Marten himself was dropped from the Council, and did not regain a place on it until November 1651. No doubt it was the Presbyterian grandees who kept him off, with their obsessive fear of religious toleration – understandable enough when one considers the proliferation of lunatic, lower-class sects. This was the consequence of overturning the Church; by 1660 many of them had learned their lesson. It was such powerful types as Sir Arthur Heselrig who managed to defeat the reforms proposed by Marten's left-wing group – Heselrig had made a fortune out of the war, installing himself in the Bishop of Durham's Auckland Castle.

Marten's gang were a rather distinguished group of intellectuals, university men, mostly unbelieving and free in their morals. Thomas Chaloner was another Oxford man, 'as far from a Puritan as the East from the West. He was of the natural religion, and of Henry Marten's gang, and one who enjoyed the pleasures of this life. He was, they say, a good scholar ... wrote an anonymous pamphlet, *An Account of the Discovery of Moses's Tomb*, which was written very wittily. It did set the wits of all the rabbis of the Assembly [i.e. the divines of the Presbyterian Westminster Assembly] then to work, and 'twas a pretty while before the sham was detected.' – Just the kind of joke to play upon those wiseacres. But he had secular tricks to take in other fools too. He would go down to Westminster Hall of a morning to let off some absurd story, and return a few hours later to note how it had spread and grown among the credulous people.

An intimate associate was Thomas May, poet and historian. 'His translation of Lucan's excellent poem made him in love with the republic, which tang stuck by him.' He was a handsome man, but 'debauched *ad omnia*' and 'would, when *inter pocula*, [i.e. in his cups], speak slightingly of the Trinity'. He wrote a good many books and stood candidate for Poet Laureate after Ben Jonson, but Sir William Davenant carried it away. Aubrey sums up succinctly: 'Clap. Came of his death after drinking with his chin tied with his cap, being fat: suffocated.' The great Lord Chatham considered his *History of the Long Parliament* 'honester and more instructive than Clarendon's'; but that was a Whig view.

Henry Neville, another Oxford man, was a Berkshire neighbour of Marten's and more of a pure doctrinaire. He was with Marten on the Council of State in 1651, and ceased to be a political figure with him when Cromwell sent the Rump packing in April 1653. Besides writing irreligious lampoons to vex the Saints he wrote a rebarbative work of political theory, *Plato Redivivus: a Dialogue concerning Government*, which much impressed Hobbes, not much given to being impressed by others. These people were free-thinking rationalists; what vitiated their politics and rendered their thought nugatory was the simple fact that people are not rational or capable of thinking, strictly speaking.

Professor Worden points out the contradiction within the Puritan Revolution between 'spiritual [sc. religious] and secular radicalism. Had the Civil War been fought, as the sects believed, on behalf of the godly elect? Or had its outcome, as Marten and Chaloner argued, been the victory of popular political rights?'[1] The short answer is – neither: it had been a conflict for power and place, between two

[1] Blair Worden, *The Rump Parliament, 1648-1653*, 260.

sections of the governing class. The rift between religious and political aims was nowhere more graphically revealed or expressed than in the all too public soul-searchings of Oliver Cromwell: he was really no revolutionary except for his religious beliefs, and much of his career was an heroic attempt to bridge the gap between his political horse-sense and his hysterical religiosity.

Disillusioned with their efforts at reforms of any kind, for even in the Rump of no more than a hundred and fifty MPs, Marten's gang was only a small minority against the embattled block of property owners, hard-faced men who had done well out of the war, he and his friends turned their attention to commercial and foreign affairs – they had connexions in the City. In November 1652 Marten, Chaloner and Neville captured the committees for the navy and foreign affairs, while the commercial interests were behind the war with the Dutch. Success in war tended, as frequently in history, to put national sentiment at the service of the revolution, and Marten and his friends saw the first Dutch war as a triumph for Parliament. Cromwell, for religious reasons, favoured peace with Holland.

Conversely, reverses at sea provoked criticism of the Rump's committee responsible for the navy. Disillusionment spread, Parliamentary attendance dropped. The administrative competence of a Parliamentary committee to conduct a war was challenged; the navy committee was replaced by commissioners, Marten and Neville lost their places on the Council of State. Their careers as politicians possessing power – what politicians are for – were ended. It was a portent of more drastic change: the days of the Republic were numbered.

It was brought to an end by Oliver Cromwell sending Parliament – the Rump that was left of it – packing in April 1653. He and the Army had had enough of it – let alone the country at large, which saw its humiliating dismissal without regret, while the defeated Royalists openly rejoiced. Was this what the Civil War had been fought for, thousands of men killed, untold destruction and waste of the country's resources, the sale and dispersal of its treasures? (Few, only the elect, minded about them.) The question at issue between the Parliamentarians of the Rump and their Army was whether there should not be a new Parliament elected to give something of a fresh mandate from the country, give it a chance to express itself, on however restricted a basis.

Cromwell and the Army wanted a new Parliament. The Parliamentary grandees, like a lot of Venetian oligarchs, wanted to prolong their own rule – it was only natural: what they had contended for all along was in fact their own self-interest and power. Some of them were prepared, as a compromise, to recruit new members to the existing depleted – and totally unrepresentative – assembly. Cromwell worked hard as usual for a compromise, and thought he had achieved an understanding; when he found that he had not and that his opponents were going back on it, he felt betrayed – and that was dangerous with such a man. It precipitated a sudden resolution.

Like Charles I in 1641 he marched down to the House – but he had the advantage of being a member, with a corps of musketeers behind him. On the morning of 20 April 1653 the Lord General, with the prestige of his victories in England, Scotland and Ireland, took his place in the Commons in a sober suit of grey with woollen stockings. For a time he listened to the members' natterings, but when the motion he disapproved was put, he rose in anger, marching up and down the floor giving vent to his pent-up indignation, disillusionment, contempt. He 'told the House that they had sat long enough unless they had done more good'. Then looking Marten and his crony Wentworth full in the face, 'some of them were whoremasters ... others of them were drunkards [this flout was for Chaloner]; some corrupt and unjust men, [so much for Heselrig and others] scandalous to the profession of the gospel. It was not fit they should sit as a Parliament any longer.' When members dared to protest, he called in his musketeers, forced the Speaker from his chair, and cleared the House. Spying the Speaker's mace lying on the table, he called to one of his soldiers, 'Take away that fool's bauble.' He remained in the House till the last member had gone, then shut the doors and locked them up.

Some memory of that earlier scene twelve years before must have come to mind, when the King had come down to the House and had tried all too ineffectively to procure the surrender of the Five obnoxious MPs – to find himself faced by the embattled gentlemen of England. But what a glaring contrast! Oliver was faced by a mere Rump – but it was from them that he had derived his authority: he was their General, supposedly under their orders. All the circumstances ever since 1642 were unconstitutional and revolutionary. As with all revolutions it transpired that government by committees was impossible: it needed the direction of one man. Henceforth the Lord Protector's rule was a monarchy in all but name; so long as he lived he ruled, and with far greater force and ability than Charles I had done.

It was the end of the Republic, and republicanism. As Oliver said and always held to it, 'the people were not to be trusted with their own liberty'. This was what his vehement supporter, John Milton, thought too – so what valid justification had they for overthrowing the traditional monarchy? It would return, as the country desired. Meanwhile Oliver's rule was a dictatorship, resting alone on the Army. We may leave the last word on these events to a woman, Dorothy Osborne: 'If Mr Pym were alive I wonder what he would think of these proceedings, and whether this would not appear as great a breach of the privilege of Parliament as the demanding of the Five Members.'

For Henry Marten and his friends it was the effective end

not only of their political careers but of all their deluded hopes and aspirations. And not only of them – of all the moderate Parliamentarians and Presbyterians too. Then there were the defeated Royalists, who had only to wait; for Oliver's rule, dependent on his life alone, held on in despite of the overwhelming majority of the nation, let alone of Scots and Irish.

III

We hear little of Marten during this interlude. The end of the Rump meant the end of his immunity as a debtor, and now his great failing, his extravagance, caught up with him. He had begun a rich man, but he had wasted his money on his convictions for the Good Old Cause and was now over £30,000 in debt. Others had made fortunes, like the insufferable Heselrig or the outrageous Wildman, or had done well like those holy humbugs, Stephen Marshall and Cornelius Burgess – to Milton's disgust. Marten had consistently opposed the payment of large sums to individual MPs, but such were his necessities that he had been forced to resort to Parliament himself. In June 1649 he stated his accounts, and was granted £100 a year in lieu of his arrears. In July an act was committed for settling £1,000 a year on him out of the Duke of Buckingham's confiscated lands. Later a payment of £3,000 was made to him, a repayment of a loan at a time when the Rump majority wished to seduce him away from close association with the Levellers. It was the Leveller Wildman, however, who was able to buy Marten's home, his estate at Becket; one sees the monuments of his heirs and successors, the Barringtons, promoted to the peerage, in the church at Shrivenham. Beautiful Hinton Waldrist came to another of Marten's creditors, the sensible Berkshire neighbour, John Loder, who made his fortune by attending to his business, careful farming, draining and manuring his land, increasing its productivity. Thus he paid off Henry Marten's mortgages and acquired both manors of Hinton and Longworth. (In our disastrous time the Loder family came to an end there with five sons killed by the Germans in the two wars – one sees their memorial in that church beside the moated manor-house.)

Henry – ass that he was – spent his substance not only on the Good Old Cause but on the women. Keeping his wife at Longworth, he had two establishments to maintain. Apparently there were five daughters of the marriage, and a son who died young – Henry could always be trusted to do his duty in bed; but thus the family ended. He lived mostly in London with his mistress, Mary Ward, of whom he was very fond – hence another three children. It was said that on one occasion, in the days of his prominence, at a grand masque at the Spanish ambassador's, he scandalised his respectable colleagues by giving 'chief place and respect' to his mistress, in greater finery and more bejewelled than any lady present. No wonder he was outlawed for debt in 1655, and in the next two years was confined for debt within the rules of the King's Bench prison in Southwark.

With the death of the Protector, and the fall of Tumbledown Dick Cromwell, who had none of his father's prestige or ability, a false dawn appeared for the Good Old Cause. Once more the irreparable rift between Army and Parliamentarians appeared, and both were riven by internal divisions: there was no holding things together on their basis, as General Monk, ruling in Scotland, well perceived (Milton and the doctrinaires not). When the Rump was restored in 1659 Marten resumed his seat; it was said that he was fetched from prison to make up a quorum. Then the Army turned it out, but found itself obliged to recall it, when Marten was briefly summoned to its Council of State. What did it matter? Things were breaking up; the inevitable Restoration, which the country longed for, was on its way. Monk manoeuvred it cautiously and with astonishing smoothness.

Marten perceived perfectly the way things were going, as his old Republican colleague Ludlow tells us. General Monk's 'deportment was so visible that Colonel Marten in the Parliament House resembled him to one that, being sent for to make a suit of clothes, brought with him a budget full of carpenter's tools. And being told that such things were not at all fit for the work he was desired to do, answered, "It matters not, I will do your work well enough, I warrant you." ' Ludlow continues, 'Yet for all this the pretences for a Commonwealth went never more high than at this time.' Deluded republicans, political 'thinkers' with their nostrums, theorists with their speculations met gaily for endless talky-talk at their clubs, and put forth their pamphlets by the bushel, Milton's among them. Marten's friends met in Harrington's Commonwealth Club every night in the Turk's Head tavern in New Palace Yard, under the chairmanship of Milton's pupil, Cyriack Skinner. There were Henry Neville and Wildman, some eighty of them, John Aubrey noting down the babble. Neville put forward his favourite nostrum of the ballot-box. 'The doctrine was very taking, the more because, as to human foresight [i.e. their own], there was no possibility of the King's return. But the greatest part of the Parliament-men perfectly hated this design of rotation by balloting; for they were cursed tyrants, and in love with their power.' Henry Neville proposed it in the House, but, Aubrey concludes with the old tag, whom the gods wish to destroy they first make mad. And so they chattered on to their own perdition.

The Restoration of the King in the glad Maytime of 1660 put its foot through all this nonsense, and the murderers of the King's father were at once in peril. In June a proclamation summoned the regicides to surrender, 'under pain of being excepted from any pardon' – this seemed to offer a promise of saving one's life upon surrender. Marten thereupon gave himself up, and made no attempt to fly abroad, as several of his colleagues on the court that condemned Charles I had done. But opinion mounted against the regicides, with the overwhelming Royalist reaction. Thus the Bill of Indemnity excepted Marten and eighteen others from pardon, leaving their execution suspended for the Convention Parliament to decide. Marten was left in the Tower, uncertain of his fate, but took it with his usual down-to-earth, jaunty humour. He said that 'since he had never obeyed any proclamation before, he hoped that he should not be hanged for taking the King's word now'.

In October he was brought to trial for his life at the Old Bailey; he defended himself with skill and his usual good humour, while his courage and self-possession made a favourable impression. Where some of the Puritan fanatics, like Harrison and John Carew, gloried in what they had done, Marten took a sensible and moderate line, arguing consistently that all that he had done had been done under the authority of Parliament.[2] Charged with acting maliciously in signing the King's death-warrant 'merrily and in a jesting way, as he was rallying with Lieutenant-General Cromwell', he said that that by no means implied malice. Asked if he did not repent of his part in the King's death, he pleaded judiciously that 'if it were possible for that blood to be in the veins again, *and every drop of that which was shed in the late wars*, he could wish it with all his heart'. That was politic of him, and brought out the consistency in his position, while making it appear more humane. Consistency also appeared in his willingness to submit peaceably to Charles II's government, since 'I think his Majesty that now is, is king upon the best title under heaven, for *he was called in by the representative body of England*'. This salved his conscience, for it was in keeping

[2] Cf. *An Exact and most Impartial Account of the Indictment, Arraignment, Trial and Judgment ... of Twenty Nine Regicides ...* The official account, edition of 1679.

with his democratic convictions. This was not good enough for the court, however: there was no recognition of the king's hereditary right. He was condemned to death, execution suspended.

In May 1661 the new, overwhelmingly Royalist Parliament passed a bill for executing Marten and his comrades. He was summoned to the House of Lords to be examined and give reason why execution should not take place. He pleaded his surrender upon the promise in the original Bill of Indemnity, and added good-humouredly that 'that honourable House of Commons, which he did so idolise, had given him up to death. And now this honourable House of Peers, which he had so much opposed – especially in their power of judicature – was made the sanctuary for him to fly to for his life.' Candour paid. It was said that Lord Falkland spoke up for him in the same terms in which Marten in his days of power had spoken up for Sir William Davenant: a sacrifice, according to the Law of Israel, should be without spot or blemish; 'and now you are going to make an old rotten rascal a sacrifice.' Marten had good reason to appreciate the joke, for, according to Aubrey, 'this wit took in the House and saved his life'.

The rest of his life, nearly twenty years, was to be spent in perpetual imprisonment; what remained of the large estate he had inherited from his father forfeit for treason. A debt of some £2,000 to Captain Simon Musgrave was to be paid out of it – Musgrave having lost his right arm in the war. Marten's brother-in-law, Lord Lovelace, petitioned for the grant of the estate forfeited to the Crown; what was left of it was so heavily encumbered with mortgages that it was of little profit to the Crown or the Duke of York to whom it was granted. Lovelace said that he had been friendly with Henry in his younger days and had become surety for him for £12,000, though he held recognisances for only £8,000. One fragment of flotsam turns up from the ruin of that handsome estate in Berkshire – the presentation to the rectory of Ashbury, in the King's gift by Marten's attainder.

In July 1662 a warrant went out to Sir John Robinson, Lieutenant of the Tower – nephew and heir of Archbishop Laud who had been done to death there (such was the *bouleversement*) – to deliver Marten to Captain Lambert of the *Anne* for transporting him to Berwick, where he was imprisoned for the next two years. In 1665 he was conveyed to Windsor Castle, until Charles II could no longer bear the sight of him walking on the leads and had him sent in 1668 to Chepstow Castle, where he remained till his death.

At salubrious Chepstow, overlooking the Wye, one can still see Marten's Tower where he was confined – not harshly, for he was allowed out to dine occasionally at a house in the vicinity, where he gave his portrait to his host. When he died in 1680, he was at first buried in the chancel of the church, appropriately for a personage of his importance – later moved to the back of the church, more appropriately for an unbeliever. He had had plenty of time to write his own epitaph:

Henry Marten here was buried September 9th 1680:

> A trueborn Englishman
> Who in Berkshire was well known
> To love his country's freedom 'bove his own,
> But being immured full twenty year
> Had time to write as doth appear
> His epitaph.

There follow some anagrammatic doggerel verses assuring the reader that

> My time was spent in serving you and you
> And death's my pay it seems, and welcome too.

He does not disturb the consistency of his belief by any future hopes:

Here or elsewhere all's one to you or me
Earth, air or water grips my ghostly dust
None know how soon to be by fire set free.

He ends by bidding the reader take care

Not how you end but how you spend your days.

He can hardly have thought that his own had been well spent, though many good deeds can be attributed to him. In 1647 he and the great Selden had moved a motion for the toleration of Catholics. Marten felt that the Irish should be left free to practise Popery, if they wished – and indeed that would have saved a lot of trouble. He was equally tolerant about the Quakers, whose oddities alarmed and offended everybody. He had also proposed the re-admission of the Jews to England, and we know of his measure for the relief of poor debtors from prison – a measure from which he had gained no relief himself.

Professor C.M. Williams has brought to light some of Marten's interventions on behalf of poor people, besides those for the well known like Sir William Davenant and Lilburne, the poet Waller and the Earl of Rutland. 'It was to Marten that the exiled Lilburne wrote seeking for help for wounded English sailors he had found abandoned in Zealand. He counted on a sympathetic response ... So did the widow Ellen Benson when one child died and another was starving at her breast; and hard-pressed Anne Windsor when the state did not honour the debentures of her husband away fighting in Scotland; and many handicraft men, widows and servants who had lent money to the Parliament and discovered that they were to be left in the lurch while rich creditors were to be paid.'

Henry Marten was of unimpeachable good nature – except where kings were concerned. There is something disarming about someone who could say of himself that

3. Henry Marten: Republican and Regicide

having attacked King, Scots, Lord Mayors and Aldermen, the Assembly of Divines, House of Lords and most of the Commons, he 'could not but expect to be reproached and inveighed against by almost every pen and tongue that would take notice of so mean a subject.'

Indeed, he was singularly disinterested, not only for that age when everybody fought for his own self-interest, but for a politician at any time. Honest Aubrey pays tribute to this quality that shone out in him: 'he was a great and faithful lover of his country, and never got a farthing by the Parliament. He was of an incomparable wit for repartees; not at all covetous; humble, not at all arrogant, as most of them were; a great cultor of justice, and did always in the House take the part of the oppressed ... He was very hospitable and exceeding popular in Berkshire, the whole county.' So he got what he deserved.

Many of his turns of wit circulated and were remembered. 'A godly member made a motion to have all profane and unsanctified persons expelled the House. Henry Marten stood up and moved that all the fools might be put out likewise, and then there would be a thin House.' He was apt, like another clever Parliamentarian subsequently – Lord North – to pretend to sleep, and then catch someone out who thought he was nodding. 'Oliver Cromwell once in the House called him, jestingly or scoffingly, "Sir Harry Marten". Henry Marten rises and bows: "I thank your Majesty, I always thought when you were king that I should be knighted." ' Cromwell was on his way to becoming king all right: no knighthood for a politician totally without humbug. But that he possessed a measure of wisdom appeared from what he wrote of Charles I to a Berkshire cousin, that 'if his Majesty should take advice of his gunsmiths and powder-men, he would never have peace'. This was precisely what the royalist Clarendon thought – Charles I had a fatal habit of listening to bad advice. And Clarendon, no admirer, gives an example of the way Marten had – like Selden – of quoting Scripture to the Saints to their confusion. He made a famous speech when the Republic was tottering to its end at the hands of Cromwell, comparing it to the infant Moses nursed by Pharaoh's daughter, and how they should be careful to nurse the Commonwealth as 'yet an infant, of a weak growth and a very tender constitution ... They should not think of putting it under any other hands until it had obtained more years and vigour. To which he added that they had another infant too, which was the war with Holland, which had thrived wonderfully under their conduct; he much doubted that it would be quickly strangled if it were taken out of their care who had hitherto governed it.' Cromwell ended both.

Marten was a patriot, whose best political pamphlet was written in 1647 to assert 'The Independency of England endeavoured to be maintained against the Claims of the Scots Commissioners'. This was praised by John Forster 'for closeness of reasoning, familiar wit of illustration, and conciseness of style ... quite worthy of Swift' – high praise for him, if somewhat exaggerated to us. Another congenial pamphlet was written in reproof of the nauseatingly self-righteous Prynne. It must have given Marten pleasure to point out the obvious truth that both Presbyterians and Independents were heretics in the eyes of the Church, and that all that men clamoured about God was only Opinion – just what the great Selden said.

We cannot but prefer to his politicising the love letters which Marten wrote to his mistress when incarcerated in the Tower, with the prospect of execution before him. They exhibit – besides courage, philosophy, stoicism – love as well as good nature; when a 'respectable' Puritan like Prynne had not a spark of love or good nature in him. Henry writes: 'My own heart, This keeper of mine is a very civil person to me when he is with me, and swears he will visit thee and bring thee to me whatever it costs ... So

Goodmorrow to my own sweet dear, thine yet and yet and yet.' Next, though he has not a penny in his purse, he sends 'his Love something that may be reasonable good: the roots come from Colchester and the water with a little sugar tastes not ill. God be with my poor heart and all the little pieces thereof. Thine everlastingly ...' It would seem that at length his heart had become fixed upon this poor young woman.

'My Heart, It was late this morning ere I received thy yesterday's basket and letter, the sweetest flower in the basket. At last Mr Loder [his creditor who succeeded to lovely Hinton Waldrist] has come to town and I think will let me see him tomorrow. My keeper and I are contriving how I may see somebody else, but I will not tell thee who that is because thou hast a shrewd guess of thine own. I have sent thee two Tower loaves of two sorts and every money I have. 'Twill mend and so will Thine own ...'

It seems that the young woman was with child again. 'My Sweet Soul, Yea, but I will see my own dear tomorrow and all my little bantlings; for the Gentleman Porter has picked out that time to grant me thy company when Sir John is sure to dine abroad, for he must not know it. I do not know whether thou darest venture thy baby upon the water or no, but the tide serves finely between 11 and 12. If thou comest by coach (which I think is the safest way) thou must set out an hour sooner, or else I shall eat up all the victuals before thou comest.' In the next we come closest to their relations and the contingencies of that dangerous time. 'My Sweet Love, Though I burnt thy letter so soon as I had read it, according to thy order, yet I have not forgotten the contents of it. Concerning the offer thou hadst of a new dear, there was a time, I confess, when I was such a hog to think my throat cut by anybody that would have a share in thee besides myself. I am reformed – but not the ordinary way by not caring ... I relish thy happiness beyond my own: if it were not for fear of seeming to compliment, I would tell thee that I would not live. I am sure I would not beg to live, but because I find thou wouldst have me live, therefore, good Soul ... study how to satisfy thy own mind and there lie I as quiet as a lamb. My poor heart, take heed of everybody, especially of the fairest offers: thou hast been bitten, and bitten and bitten by such as were not mere strangers to thee. By that time thou art a little older thou wilt take every word thou hearest for an arrant lie, the world has grown so false ... My dearest, Thy everlasting self, Henry Marten.'

At last his fate was to be decided. 'My sweet dear, brave gallant soul, Now stand thy ground, I was told on Tuesday night that the House of Commons had given us all up on Monday and had appointed a Committee to bring in a bill for that purpose, which cannot require much time. And if I wish anything in the world it is that thou hadst been with me when the tidings came, and ever since to see if thou couldst find any alteration in me sleeping or waking ...' He could not tell how things would work out, or what his fate would be. 'He that has time has life: a thousand things happen betwixt the cup and the lip, and it is some comfort that we can still send to each other. I was not so hasty to send thee this news yesterday, but I was afraid thou wouldst hear it from another hand, that would make it worse. Pluck up thy strength, my good heart, conquer this brunt and thou art a man for ever. Look upon thy little brats and see if thy dear be not amongst them. Has not one of 'em his face, another his brain, another his mirth? And look thou most upon that, for it is just the best thing in this world, and a thing that could not be taken from him when all the remainder of my estate and thine was; not when my liberty and the assurance of my life was, nor when thy company was, which though I reckon last goes for something with, my dearest Dear, Thine own own, Henry Marten.'

In these letters one penetrates at last to what kind of

man Henry Marten really was at heart. The world saw only the exterior, the politician, the wit, the regicide. All the same, for all the charm and spirit, one cannot help wondering what became of the poor young woman and her children, and at the bravery of women in committing their fate to such men.

We may conclude that Marten was betrayed by the one element of faith this otherwise rational man had – faith in the people.

Chief sources: *Cal. State Papers Domestic*; Bulstrode Whitelocke, *Memorials of the English Affairs*, 4 vols; John Aubrey, *Brief Lives*, ed. A. Clark, 2 vols; Edmund Ludlow, *Memoirs*, 2 vols, ed. C.H. Firth; Clarendon, *History of the Great Rebellion; Mercurius Aulicus*, reprinted in *The English Revolution. Newsbooks*, 4 vols; Nicholas Davenport, *The Honour of St Valery: The Story of an English Manor House; Dictionary of National Biography*, article by C.H. Firth; C.M. Williams, 'The Anatomy of a Radical Gentleman: Henry Marten', in *Puritans and Revolutionaries*, ed. by D. Pennington and K. Thomas.

CHAPTER 4

Hugh Peters: Puritan Propagandist and Coloniser

Hugh Peters was about the most vilified man in the whole Civil War period, not only by Royalists but by Presbyterians like Edwards of the suitably entitled *Gangraena* and the vitriolic Prynne, from within his own community of the Saints. For he was one of the Saints, an Independent, i.e. in modern terms a Congregationalist, very close to Oliver Cromwell, whose army chaplain he was. As such he was the most popular of Puritan preachers, speaking straight to the people in their own homely terms, with a good deal of play-acting and bufoonery. It was very effective, more so than the elaborate Biblical disquisitions of orthodox Presbyterian divines – like his cousin Charles Herle, for example, Prolocutor of the Westminster Assembly.

Yet there was much more to Hugh Peters than this. He had a noteworthy career in New England, not only in his successful ministry at Salem but in his energetic stimulation of the fisheries, the impulse he gave to manufactures, trade and colonising enterprise. He had immense energy, which kept him perpetually on the move, between England and Holland – with which he advocated peace against the war waged by the Commonwealth; between Wales and Ireland; propagating the Puritan cause all over southern England, accompanying the army on its marches, inspiriting the soldiers with his talks, often comic turns; a favourite preacher in London, preaching hundreds of sermons; chaplain to the Commonwealth's Council of State; reporting the victories in the field to the House of Commons at Westminster; the leading member of Cromwell's Committee of Triers, to test and appoint ministers to parishes all over England, with apartments in Whitehall Palace, a kind of Cromwellian Archbishop of Canterbury, as he was hailed.

He ended on the gallows at Charing Cross, hanged as a regicide, which he was not. Some regicides, who had influence behind them and powerful personages to speak up for them, escaped the gallows – Colonel Hutchinson for one, Henry Marten for another. Hugh Peters had no one to speak up for him. No one had a good word to say for him, though he had done plenty of good works in his busy, meddling life. He was not a bad fellow.

We must confront at once the worst about him. Though he was not a member of the court that 'tried' the King and was not present at his execution – people even said that he was the masked executioner! – he preached up the King's being brought to 'trial'. That was bad enough. Milton was just as blameworthy, who justified the public murder before European opinion; but he escaped justice, after a short imprisonment. The mob, which had enjoyed Peters' preaching, howled for his blood. Though a Puritan is not quite my cup of tea, we must be just to him.

What was he really like?

He was a sort of Revivalist preacher, such as we were familiar with in old days in Cornwall. He was an enthusiast who could rouse an audience to fervour, and in the Civil War he became a rabble-rouser. He was full of good works himself, for ever meddling with other people's business; but then he had business ability, inherited from his family on both sides. He was actively charitable, and made it his concern to help the poor and always speak up for them. He was even rather tolerant, within the Puritan fold, of course – like Cromwell, with whom he had something in common – though that meant excluding actual Anglicans and Papists.

What he had in common with Cromwell was a vein of religious hysteria; both were manic-depressives, exhibiting demonic energy in their manic phase, but suffering doubt and depression at intervals. Both of them had nervous breakdowns, Peters more than once. Exceptional men, they had exceptional energy and initiative. Cromwell evidently trusted Peters, and Peters could always be found on Cromwell's side. They spoke the same horrid Biblical language; both were opportunists, practical men, Cromwell with instinctive genius for seizing the initiative. Both were gentlemen – Cromwell indeed an aristocrat with his connexions in the peerage (like a Roosevelt leading the New Deal); while Peters came from good family.

His stock was curiously mixed – Dutch, English, Cornish – and that inheritance must account for his make-up. He had what may be described as a Celtic temperament – emotional, intense, very personal and jumpy, impulsive and warm-hearted, kindly, except where his prejudices were concerned. The top dressing – what the Germans call *Bildung* – was English, the intellectual outfit of Cambridge Puritanism. Then there was the Dutch side – his affiliations with Holland were strongly marked; his business ability and practical capacity may have come mainly from there.

There has been some confusion and dispute about Peters' paternal ancestry; but it can be said definitely that the family had nothing to do with the Devonshire family of Petre, which made its fortune out of the Dissolution of the monasteries yet went on being Catholic, as they still are today. Hugh Peters was baptised at Fowey, on 11 June 1598, of a Protestant family from the Netherlands known as Dickwood, i.e. Dyckveldt. Two brothers, traders, settled in Fowey towards the end of Henry VIII's reign and shared in the expanding prosperity the port enjoyed in the Elizabethan age. After the medieval Treffry family, in their grand mansion of Place overlooking town and harbour, and the Rashleigh newcomers from Devon, these Dickwoods were the leading traders and shipowners in the town. From their wills, with their bequests of silver, plate and property, and from their marriages into the Cornish gentry, it is evident that they were well-to-do and accepted as social equals.

At some point they took the convenient alias of Peters, a common enough name in Cornwall, through some connexion as to which there is no evidence. Thomas Peters' elder son, Thomas, married John Treffry's daughter, Martha, in 1594. Their son, to become so notorious, was born probably at the pretty farm of Hill Hay, in its sequestered valley just outside the town. Eventually Hugh inherited it – a few of the old walls of the southward looking farmhouse (still belonging to the Treffrys) would go back to his days. A sister of Martha Treffry married Edward Herle of beautiful Prideaux at the mouth of Luxulyan Valley, and became the mother of Charles Herle, rector of the fattest living in Lancashire, Winwick, and the author of fat tomes of senseless divinity. Another Treffry daughter, Deborah, married another Peters uncle, Henry, MP for Fowey in 1610.

Hugh's mother died in the year of his birth, perhaps in childbirth; his father's second marriage produced so many children as to clog his affairs – or they went down with the decline of Fowey's prosperity. A half-brother of Hugh, Benjamin (called after Benjamin Treffry), became a well-known ship's master and commanded the little fleet that carried Hugh over to combat the Irish Rebellion in 1641. Other marriages knit the Peterses into the Cornish gentry and into the Church. A cousin of Hugh, Jane Treffry, married the head of the Trefusis family, a Parliamentarian – by no means all Cornish families were

Royalist. Hugh's brother, Thomas, became vicar of Mylor. During a spell in New England Thomas married a sister of Governor John Winthrop, senior; Hugh's step-daughter married John Winthrop, junior.

All these people ranked as gentry. The most unrespectable member of this spreading connexion had a respectable background. As he wrote himself in the last of his many writings, *A Dying Father's Last Legacy*, from the Tower of London facing death: 'I was the son of considerable parents from Foy[1] in Cornwall, my father a merchant, his ancestors driven thither from Antwerp for religion – I mean the Reformed; my mother of the same town, of a very ancient family, the name Treffry of Place, or the Place in that town, of which I would not boast.'

Hugh went up in 1613 as a sizar to Trinity College, Cambridge, where he served one Norris. It is typical of his kindly impulses that, when he was a Trier in power, he enabled Norris to keep his living though devoted to the Prayer Book. His university career was undistinguished; he never became an intellectual, and it is a recommendation of him that he never added to the graceless burden of Puritan theology. However, his mind was formed by the Puritanism dominant at Cambridge, and the adjurations of Gouge, Sibbes and such. It was some years since the revered Perkins had been roaring away in St Mary's, giving the congregation a thrill with his favourite iteration of the word 'Damned'; but his books were best-sellers, a formative influence on many minds.

Peters was to find his forte – and ultimate damnation – in preaching too. But first he had to undergo the thrill of conversion, as the result of a sermon he heard 'under Paul's', presumably at St Paul's Cross (note the Puritan

---

[1] This is how Fowey is pronounced and it would be sensible to revert to the old spelling. Place – as at Place, Padstow, and Place at St Anthony in Roseland – refers to the place, or monastic tithe-barn, which dominated the medieval economic life of the place.

omission of the 'Saint'). He got a job as a schoolmaster in Essex, was ordained and received a licence to preach as a curate at Rayleigh. Here he attracted the patronage of the Earl of Warwick, a magnate of the Rich family, whose enormous fortune was made by the Rich lawyer who perjured himself to bring Sir Thomas More to the scaffold, yet died a Catholic in the reign of Elizabeth. The Riches, like Pym and other Puritans were empire-builders, involved in the colonisation of New England. Peters equipped himself with a wife by sensibly marrying a well-endowed Essex widow, Mrs Reade, a 'good gentlewoman', thus extending his connexions in that godly area.

Meanwhile, he was making a name for himself as one of the popular unbeneficed 'Lecturers', supported by the laity, who gave Archbishop Laud so much trouble. Peters estimated attendance at his sermons in St Sepulchre's, Holborn – as did John Wesley his in the open air – in thousands, when they were more likely hundreds. At a public fast ordained by Warwick Peters prayed for 'the Queen that God would remove from her the idols of her father's house, and that she would forsake the idolatry and superstition wherein she was bred and must needs perish if she continued in the same'. It would have been enormous political help, and a comfort to Charles I, if she had put away her nonsense and conformed – but it was not for Peters to say so. Not unnaturally his licence to preach was suspended. He spent his time collecting money for the lay feoffees engaged in buying up advowsons (presentations) to livings, to put in Puritans they approved of – another headache for poor Archbishop Laud. Peters developed a talent as a collector of money for such nuisances. Shortly he became a stockholder in the New England Company, which encouraged the mass emigration of the 1630s that made New England what it became.

Having attracted unfavourable notice in England Peters betook himself to the Netherlands. He had his first experience as an army chaplain serving with the English regiments under Dutch command; in his report of their successes he saw, of course, 'the hand of God'. Here was another apprenticeship that he was serving; though he failed to establish himself in the English church at Amsterdam, where the pastor was a Presbyterian with a strong antipathy to Independents. Hugh got a temporary job with William Ames, whose theological works exercised such influence among the godly of New England. When the sainted Ames died, Peters wrapped himself in the departed's cloak to gain inspiration – a gesture which became characteristic of his later pulpit tricks.

At length he got the pastorship of the English church at Rotterdam. After some disputes with the Presbyterians he managed to exclude them and base the church on its own exclusive covenant of grace, i.e. a congregational bottom. In England he had testified to his bishop, 'for the Church of England (I bless God) I am a member of it, and was baptised in it, and am not only assured it is a true Church, but am persuaded it is the most glorious and flourishing this day under the sun; and for the faith, doctrine and articles of that Church, and the maintenance of them, I hope the Lord will enable me to contend. Yea, I trust to lay down my life, if I were called thereunto.' This was said with his usual exaggeration, but the foundation of the English church was not Congregational and, when Peters was called to lay down his life, it was not for the Church.

The authorities in England disapproved of the independent doings of their churches in the Netherlands and at length reduced them to order, insisting on conformity with the Prayer Book. After seven years in the country with which he had an inherited affinity he had to look elsewhere. Where but to their New Jerusalem, New England? As one of the East Anglian brethren said: 'Religion stands on tiptoe in this land, looking westwards.' By 'religion' they meant their own, of course – as everybody else did.

The emigration *en masse* was in full flood in the 1630s, and Peters sailed in the *Abigail*, with John Winthrop junior, and the younger Henry Vane who became briefly governor of Massachusetts, until he quarrelled with the godly and went home. Peters' first posting was as agent for the plantation at Saybrook, Connecticut, but he made himself extremely useful throughout the settlements. 'In 1636, by travelling from place to place and giving propaganda speeches in public and in private, he had stimulated the public to contribute a considerable sum with which a magazine of fishing provisions was established. Reasonable prices replaced exorbitant profiteering, and the fishing industry prospered.' He followed this up by stimulating a shipbuilding industry, prime manufactures and trade, buying supplies abroad, importing saltpetre for gunpowder from Holland. Governor Winthrop paid tribute to his manic energy, and Peters helped in other ways too, adjusting factions left in the wake of the insufferable Vane, for the godly quarrelled like mad.

Especially the minister at Salem, Roger Williams, favoured with a special dispensation of the 'truth', though he could not agree with himself about it for long, let alone with anybody else. Quarrelling with Thomas Hooker, who enjoyed a certain spiritual primacy, Williams raised a storm in the colony, shook the dust off his feet and departed from Massachusetts. Peters took his place at Salem, with general agreement, laying on of hands, etc. There he was successful, after separating out those who disagreed – fissiparous separating was a vocational disease with the Saints, as later with the Methodists.

Trouble was caused by the tiresome Mrs Hutchinson, with her revelations from on high; she naturally recruited followers, for they had an 'immediate revelation in an absolute promise from God'. The orthodox were in error, under a covenant of 'works' instead of faith and grace. It is amusing to see the old quarrel between Protestantism and

Catholicism recapitulated in microcosm here, and ironical
to see Peters forced into Archbishop Laud's part, having to
defend the majority institution as a social rampart against
the antinomianism of a small minority of dissidents. Peters
was not responsible for the persecution of this irrepressible
woman, but he had to take part in it. She was driven out
into the wilderness, which was the place for her, and was
eventually murdered by Indians.

As minister Peters enforced Congregationalist orthodoxy
– one is reminded of Chesterton's 'Orthodoxy is my doxy;
heterodoxy other people's doxy'. Separatists who wanted to
go their own way were excommunicated; if this was
necessary in New England, still more so was it in Old
England. With the inpouring of immigrants Peters'
congregation grew, his ministry prospered. His energy
knew no bounds: negotiations with the Dutch East India
Company, with the other settlements – trying to head off
the heretical Roger Williams from settling Narragansett
Bay; laying the groundwork for trade with the West Indies,
which was to be a foundation of New England's prosperity.
In all this Peters' business acumen was to the fore. Hardly
less active was his charitable spirit; he was one of the
foremost in founding Harvard College, collecting money for
books and a scholarship which is still in existence.

Trouble came from his private life. His wife came over
and shortly died. He was not long in looking round for a
new one – and caught a tartar, another widow, Mrs
Deliverance Sheffield, from whom, before the knot was tied,
he was already seeking deliverance. The woman was a
known neurotic, but neither her family nor the congregation would let their pastor off the hook. He wrote to
Governor Winthrop: 'Good sir, let me not be a fool in Israel.
You have often said that I could not leave her; what to do is
very considerable. Could I with comfort and credit desist,
this seems best.' He could not: he became a fool in Israel.
He married her and, after the birth of a child, she went off

her head; the godly interpreted this to mean that she was possessed of the Devil, excommunicated her, and sent her after Hugh, who had by now escaped to England.

His biographer sums up that 'his years in New England (1635-1641) were the most active and, on the whole, the most constructive years of his life. As a promoter of the public interest he was unsurpassed in New England at the time. He was primarily interested in placing the Bay Colony on a basis as nearly self-sufficing as possible. It is doubtful whether he ever looked upon New England as a colony: it was a commonwealth of the godly dedicated to the principles of the Word and to the polity of the primitive churches of Christ.'

In 1641, with the collapse of Charles and Laud's government, promising prospects opened up in England. Peters was rewarded for his services in the colony with grants of land and cash; he retained his link, for he went home as agent for Massachusetts. In the years that followed his relations with the godly there ran on the rocks. In the first place came disagreement over religion. Peters did not hold with the persecuting ways of the Bible Commonwealth, the 'city set as it were upon an hill' – for other less enlightened folk to follow, otherwise out they went. Dissensions even sprang up among themselves: he wrote back, in the language of Puritan cant, 'Ah, sweet New England! and yet sweeter if divisions be not among you, if you will give any encouragement to those that are godly and shall differ, etc.' More important was financial and business disagreement. With transactions at such a distance, all the delays and losses in crossing the Atlantic, cash disappeared and accounts were muddled. Peters and his colleague as agent were charged with peculation and annexing funds they collected. It is unlikely that Peters was guilty; he had independent sources of income, and meanwhile was losing on his property left behind there.

Henceforward he had more important things to do: he

was caught up in the excitement of the Puritan Revolution at home. The Irish rebellion of 1641, and the massacre of the English and Scottish settlers that followed, generated an intense reaction in England, with a Puritan determination to avenge it. This was heralded by a small expedition that year under a Scot, Lord Forbes; the ships commanded by Benjamin Peters, with Hugh to preach it up. Too small to effect anything to the purpose, Peters nevertheless gave an enthusiastic report of its doings to Parliament – the beginning of his career as promoter of the Good Old Cause. It was followed later by energetic tours, 'roaring it up and down the country'. He took the line of no compromise with the King and preached against any negotiations; like Cromwell, who was in favour of fighting to a victorious conclusion. Then what? This already foreshadowed a rift with the Presbyterian Parliamentarians, whose line was a riddle – protested a soldier – 'our fighting against the King and yet fighting for him'.

Meanwhile the New England Saints were going at it hammer and tongs. It fell to Peters in 1643 to put together their statements and queries and rejoinders – Richard Mather versus John Davenport, etc. – in a publication of which we may judge the value from the title: *Church-Government and Church-Covenant Discussed: In an Answer of the Elders of the several Churches in New England to Two and thirty Questions, sent over to them by divers Ministers in England, to declare their judgements therein. Together with an Apology of the said Elders in New England for the Church-Covenant, sent over to Master Bernard in 1639. As also in Answer to nine Positions about Church-Government. And now published for the satisfaction of all who desire resolution in these points.* So far from it satisfying anybody it produced further controversy; nobody believed Peters' assurance that Independents sought no mastery. Both wanted to get on top.

How it makes one sympathise with Laud! The poor

Archbishop, who had gone on working in the Tower, in danger of being forgotten, was now brought to trial to please the Scotch Presbyterians. The papers which he needed for his defence were ransacked, and some abstracted, by the vengeful Prynne hounding on the trial: *Canterbury's Doom* as his voluminous folio pronounced it, for the result was a foregone conclusion. Laud defended himself with honesty and ability – all that he had done had been in accordance with the law. He enraged his persecutors by his claim that he had reconciled at least twenty persons, some of great eminence, to Protestantism: 'let any clergyman of England come forth and give a better account of his zeal to the present Church.' 'Zeal' was a Puritan cant-word. 'What put them into this choler I know not, unless they were angry to hear me say so much in my own defence – especially for the conversion of so many, which I think they little expected.' Unable to prove Laud guilty of anything against the state, they fell back upon attainder, as with Strafford, i.e. murder by executive decision.

Peters played a sorry part in this – it is one of the worst counts against him. From the court 'Mr Peters followed me in great haste and began to give me ill language, and told me that he and other ministers were able to name thousands that they had converted'. Typical exaggeration – but this was what had nettled them, and the Archbishop was able to name his converts. As for Peters, 'I knew him not, as never having seen him in my life, though I had heard enough of him'. On the way to the scaffold Peters hung upon the Archbishop, old and ill, hoping to bring home to him his offences against the 'godly'.

Next year, 1644, he accompanied Essex's army into the West, as rabble-rouser to the campaign which ended in its surrender to the King in and around Fowey. Peters was on home-ground, but his preaching had no effect: Essex complained that the Cornish are 'a people as far from humanity as they are from sanctity, for they will neither serve God nor man but after the old fashion of their grandfathers, and so they make an idol of the King'. Not even Hugh's relatives, the Treffrys, were willing to go over to Parliament. He was, however, able to do them a good turn by saving their home from being ransacked, their property from depredations – unlike the Rashleighs, whose estate at Menabilly suffered heavy losses, their cattle and livestock all eaten up. As a non-combatant Peters was not taken prisoner, and by the autumn was back in London attending royalist 'delinquents' (Puritan semantics) on scaffold and gibbet, with zeal.

The year 1645 saw decisive Puritan victory in the field. Peters was present at Naseby, preaching to the troops before the battle, riding 'from rank to rank with a bible in one hand and a pistol in the other, exhorting the men to do their duty'. The victory broke the back of the Royalists militarily in the Midlands, while they remained fighting in the West. Fairfax now turned to mopping up the West, while Peters gained a permanent footing as chaplain to the New Model army. His services were indispensable, not only encouraging the troops, but addressing and bringing over the Clubmen who assembled under the threat, 'a plague on both your houses'. Passing Stonehenge Peters was shocked by 'the monuments of heathenism' and earnestly besought Fairfax to delay a day to blow them up! The Philistine Puritan provides such a contrast to John Aubrey. Others of them were desecrating the cathedrals, churches, colleges, chapels all over the country.

Peters was present at the storming of Bridgewater, praying and preaching, and performed at the solemn fast before Bristol, an orgy of prayer and exhortation. For his report to Parliament of progress in the West, he received a gratuity of £100; Oliver Cromwell £2,500 worth of lands confiscated from royalists. Basing House had been long under siege, a faithful fortress strongly held by the Catholic

Marquis of Winchester. This enraged Cromwell's soldiers in storming it, who spared not even the women flying from the walls. Basing House was really two – a medieval castle, with a splendid Elizabethan palace annexed to it. The vast complex was sacked and plundered, left a ruin. Peters described with glee the treasures accumulated there, 'the furnishings, plate, jewels, money ...' as if he had peeped into the treasures of Hell. All of it, he reported jubilantly, was sold to the country people by the soldiers, even to the lead drain pipes and gutters; the house itself demolished by fire, 'leaving nothing but bare walls and chimneys in less than twenty hours'. There is no counting the artistic losses from such destruction all over the country, the historic accumulations, portraits, pictures, archives. No historian with any aesthetic sense can but detest the Philistines who wrought it, here as elsewhere.

Peters could not refrain from taunting the old Marquis, who stood stoutly for Loyalty, which he named his house, and said that, if the King had no more ground in England, he would maintain it to the uttermost. Peters reported the triumph to the Commons: 'we see who are his majesty's dear friends, and trusty and well beloved cousins and Councillors, the Marquis being the Pope's devoted vassal.' The Castle had a crowded garrison; many of the men were trapped within the burning walls and perished: 'thus the Lord was pleased to show us how just and righteous the ways of God are, who takes sinners in their own snares, and lifteth up the heads of his despised people.'

These were 'Providences of God to the Army' – we do not know if the mysterious disease that afflicted it at Exeter was a providence too. Peters rode along with the Army and preached at Torrington, where the church happened to be blown up after the battle; on to Dartmouth and thence into Cornwall, where he was able to do good service in meeting royalist gentry and arranging east Cornwall's surrender. On Bodmin Downs he addressed a large gathering of country folk: 'I used an argument of utility, wishing them to consider how they could subsist without trade which are from the city of London and other parts of the kingdom ... Also what havoc the Irish and French might make upon them if they landed.' The argument was brought home when a ship came in at Padstow with Irish recruits for the King – most of them put to the sword.

The real argument was that Cornwall was utterly exhausted and eaten out: the gallant record of the Cornish Foot from Stratton to the capture of Bristol in 1643, their decimation and loss of their outstanding leaders; the invasion of two armies in 1644, Essex's and the King's; the retreat of the Royalist army, Fairfax upon its heels in 1645-6. Fairfax sent Peters up to Parliament with news of the final capitulation before Truro. He referred the House 'for further particulars to Master Peters, who since he came into this country [i.e. county], where he was born, both very much furthered the service in bringing of the country in so freely to the protection of Parliament'. Since the issue was settled, we may put this service down to the credit side of his account. The Commons ordered him a reward of lands to the value of £200 a year, out of the Marquis of Worcester's estate; this was held up by the Presbyterian Lords, and it does not appear that Hugh got much out of it.

He celebrated this *annus mirabilis* with his best-known sermon, to both Houses of Parliament, the Lord Mayor and aldermen, and the Assembly of Divines: a grand array of coagulated Puritan notabilities. 'God's Doings and Man's Duty' was the title of this exordium. The Cause was justified by success; its victories showed God's approval: 'how the Lord hath paid them in their own coin you have many witnesses. They would have war: they have it: the sword must decide the controversy.' They could all agree to that; but a subsequent reflection can have given no pleasure to the members of the Assembly present: 'I could wish some of my learned brethren's quarrelling hours were rather spent upon clearing the originals, and so conveying over pure Scripture to posterity, than in scratching others with their sharpened pens and making cockpits of pulpits.'

We may point out in his defence that hitherto he had regularly urged concord between quarrelling Presbyterians and Independents, and had not added fuel to the flame by wrangling about theological nonsense. He was a practical man, a pragmatist. But this passage betokened his giving up hope of unity between the two parties among the godly. He had been maliciously attacked by the Presbyterians: the antiquarian-minded Prynne brought up Peters' over-enthusiastic subscription to the Church years before and published it as evidence of changeableness of mind. Another Presbyterian exposed his 'church covenants at Rotterdam and at Salem as examples of the awful consequences of setting up a church covenant distinct from the Covenant of Grace'. Insinuations were made against his morals, apparently without justification. The gangrenous Edwards held that the wife's insanity was an indication of divine displeasure. Peters rejoined by calling Edwards 'a knave and stinking fellow' – very improper from one of the Saints to another.

He was with the Army in the final stage of the siege of Oxford, and upon the surrender took part with other Independents in preaching to the unconverted. What loyalists thought about this impertinence may be seen from Anthony Wood's account after the Restoration. 'Whereas before the surrender there was no place in England more loyal to their Prince, orthodox and observant of the ceremonies of the Church of England, than the scholars and generality of Oxford were – so, after the entry of the Parliamenteers there appeared nothing but confusion, darkness, etc. Hell was broke loose upon the poor remnant, and they were overrun by sectaries, blasphemers, hypocrites, exciters to rebellion, censurers, covetous persons, men of self-pride, envy, and what not.' This tells us how Royalists felt about Puritans.

Peters stated that in the 9,000 parishes in the country there were only a thousand capable clergy. Precisely: that was the whole point of the Prayer Book and an ordered liturgy, instead of the preachments of the disordered and illiterate. Full of bright ideas as usual, he suggested that one college be devoted 'to train godly youths out of shops' to preach, i.e. like the apprentices from the City who had howled for Strafford's head, or bayed at Laud on his way to trial.

By this time Peters was recognised as 'the voice of the Army' – or the ventriloquist, we might say; 'honest' John Lilburne called him, 'a man that doth from time to time speak very much the sense of the leaders of the Army ... who lies in their bosoms and knows their secrets, and is much used by them to trumpet abroad their principles and tenets'. 'Used' is the word for it: we detect a certain naïveté in Peters, along with his honesty. There was no real malice in him: he didn't reflect sufficiently, borne along by his feelings and 'convictions', a cork on the current of events. He spent the rest of the year 1646 in incessant propaganda, in the Army, the City and the country. That winter he had another breakdown from over-exertion.

Conflict between the Army and Parliament was developing nicely, and the Army leaders tried to come to terms with the King. When Charles was brought to Newmarket for the purpose, in June 1647, Peters had one or two audiences of him, and kissed his hand, as a gentleman would – as Cromwell himself did. Hugh declared to his Majesty what 'a precious thing' it was for a king 'above all to be godly'. In fact Charles I was rather godly, though after a more civilised fashion. The King said, with his innate courtesy, that 'he had often heard talk of him, but did not believe he had that solidity in him he found by his discourse'. Mistaking courtesy for encouragement, Hugh asked whether the King wouldn't like to

hear him preach. His Majesty preferred to postpone that
pleasure: 'No, not as yet.'

During the Army debates at Putney, while the Levellers
and Agitators put forward their radical proposals, to the
dismay of upper-class Cromwell and Ireton, Peters was
present, preaching, praying and performing. Again when
the Army command moved to Windsor, he presided at a
solemn fast, where 'a sweet harmony' prevailed. Mr Peters
'prayed very fervently and pathetically ... this continued
from nine in the morning till seven at night' – just the kind
of thing to give one a nervous breakdown. A Royalist
reaction set in in the country; this, with the King's attempt
to play off Army against Parliament and bring in the Scots
again – but now on his side – flared up into the second Civil
War.

During this Peters was hard at work organising supplies
in South Wales for Cromwell to reduce Pembroke Castle.
After this, rapidly marching, Cromwell routed the Scots
under Hamilton at Preston, in which Peters saw again the
'mighty appearance of God ... I know not (almost) whether
it be not a dream'. He was able to assure the soldiery that
'he had found, upon a strict scrutiny, that there were in the
Army 5,000 Saints, no less holy than now conversed in
heaven with God Almighty'. Stripped of its nonsense, this
means that he calculated there were 5,000 supporters of
Independency. At Windsor the Army leaders argued out
what they were to do with the King, whom they blamed for
the renewal of war; their soldiers, after all the propaganda
against him, were demanding that he be brought to book.
Lilburne handed in a petition for Ireton to Peters, 'the
grand Journey- or Hackney-man of the Army'.

He moved with them to London, and was present when
the Army put through its purge of the Presbyterians in
Parliament – now, too late, anxious for accommodation
with the King. When these prominent MPs asked by what
authority they were thus extinguished, quite put out,

Peters replied with naif candour: 'By the power of the sword.' Cromwell the politician would not have blurted that out; he would have veiled it with religious cant. We may quote one example of Peters' pulpit technique, preaching at St Margaret's Westminster before the King's 'trial'. He was acting the subject of Moses leading the Israelites out of their Egyptian bondage, and applying the moral to the Army leaders. ' "But how must this be done? That is not yet revealed unto me!" quoth Hugh. Then, covering his eyes with his hands and laying down his head on the cushion – until the people falling into a laughter, awakened him – he started up and cried out: "Now I have it by revelation – now I shall tell you: This Army must root up monarchy ... this is to bring you out of Egypt." '

Puritan congregations, the theatre having been suppressed, preferred this kind of buffoonery. Hugh Peters was to pay a terrible price for his antics in the end. Before his execution he confessed to his daughter his regret that he had ever been 'popular' – the word had a stronger meaning then: it meant, lowering himself to the level of the populace. But the ventriloquist was merely expressing the decision in the minds of the Army leaders to get rid of the King. When Charles was brought to London for 'trial', Peters was sent, with two other Independent chaplains, to escort him – Hugh riding before his coach 'like a bishop-almoner ... triumphing'.

He was present also at the shameful scene in Westminster Hall, congratulating Bradshaw, 'This is a most glorious beginning of the work.' He urged on the members of the court by preaching and prayer: 'Whoso sheddeth man's blood, by man shall his blood be shed.' Propaganda placed all the blame for what had happened on one man's shoulders; and Biblical texts were ready to hand from the savage Old Testament to preach up the King's execution. Peters was not a member of the court, and so technically was not a regicide. On the day of the King's execution he was away ill; but he was now so notorious a figure that the rumour spread that he was the masked executioner.

When his turn came, he was condemned for inciting the King's death. Was Milton any better, who defended it after the event?

In that fatal year 1649 Hugh Peters suffered a breakdown twice, from the excitement and strain of it all. On the second occasion he had a better excuse: his wife, from whom he had freed himself once, had gone insane again in Massachusetts, whence the godly shipped her back home to him: Deliverance Peters.

Now came the reckoning with the Irish for the massacre of 1641. On his recovery Hugh was employed in South Wales organising supplies in Milford Haven for Cromwell's retaliatory expedition: 'I never saw the seamen in so unanimous and gallant a posture, and indeed knowing in the things of God.' On Cromwell's return from Drogheda to Dublin Hugh joined him with reinforcements for the march into Wexford: the Lord General commissioned the indispensable chaplain with the organising and business enterprise as a colonel: 'the Lord make us humble and faithful.' Once more he suffered a nervous collapse.

On his recovery and return to England he was joined to the Commissioners for the Propagation of the Gospel in Wales – an attempt to recover some of the damage done by the extrusion of the Royalist clergy. In Pembrokeshire alone some fifty had been extruded, and now there were nothing like enough ministers to fill the gap. The Puritan attempt was singularly unsuccessful, it had the effect only of eroding still further the inadequate resources of the Church in Wales. The damage the Puritan Revolution did in this quarter was permanent.[2]

---

[2] Cf. A.M. Johnson, 'Wales during the Commonwealth and Protectorate', in *Puritans and Revolutionaries*, ed. D. Pennington and K. Thomas.

4. Hugh Peters: Puritan Propagandist and Coloniser

At the end of 1650 Peters received the reward of his labours, with his appointment as a chaplain to the Council of State, apartments in Whitehall and £200 a year. For the next eight years he was in clover. A New England visitor reported his installation, 'I was merry with him and called him the Archbishop of Canterbury, in regard of his attendance by ministers and gentlemen – and it passed very well.' He was now in port and, though busy as ever, had more quiet, except for his play-acting in the pulpit. One may note the contrast with the real archbishop: Laud, whose origins as the son of a clothier were rather inferior to Peters', carried with him the dignity of the Anglican Church. Peters was exalted by the prospects of the Commonwealth: 'You are certainly on the edge of fulfilling very great and glorious prophecies,' he preached to the Rump: 'the Lord's design is the downfall of Anti-Christ.' The Puritans were able to agree who Anti-Christ was – the Pope – though unable to agree otherwise.

Now that he was on top he was attacked more scurrilously than ever, especially by Prynne. We have noted Peters' Philistinism about artistic treasures and records – he would have consigned legal antiquities to the flames in his enthusiasm for reform. Prynne, whose only good point was his care for records, replied that Peters might as well burn 'the rolls of the Old and New Testament, the ancientest of all others, which St Paul was so careful to preserve'. It would have been better for both Prynne and Peters if they had been versed in the works of Shakespeare instead – as the cultivated King was.

Peters took advantage of his new-found authority to put forward a programme of good works in his *Good Work for a Good Magistrate*. By nature a projector, his head was buzzing with schemes for improvement and plans for the Commonwealth – from a union of Protestant powers, i.e. with Holland and Sweden, down to the widening of London's streets. The universities did not escape his

117

scheming eye: they were not for 'monastic drones', each of them should contain eight colleges dedicated to training youths for the ministry, and eight for the magistracy. He was particularly concerned for the welfare of the poor; each county should provide a public stock for the encouragement of local manufactures to set them on work. Hospitals for cripples, juvenile wards for orphans, no prison for small debtors, resort to law made cheaper, antique forms abolished. Each town should have a bank for lending out, as at Amsterdam; a municipal quay for London, as in Holland; canals, dredging of rivers, marine insurance, what not.

Many of these suggestions were commonplaces of the time, others drawn from his experience of Holland. But where was the money to come from? – the country impoverished by years of civil war, plague, famine and destruction of capital, and the new Republic engaged in an adventurous foreign policy. He had some grand notion of tithes all over the country being paid into a national fund, which, after payment of a ministry, would provide revenue for schemes of improvement. They all came up against the immovable rock of custom. Neither the Commonwealth nor Cromwell's Protectorate could grapple with the religious organisation of the country, let alone the complexities of tithes, which varied from parish to parish. He was appointed to the committee to deal with reform of the law, a jungle in itself – and only a few minimal improvements emerged. Some of his suggestions were sensible – standardisation of weights and measures, for instance. Could such a scheme be envisaged, let alone enforced, in a country where these varied not only between counties but between areas within counties and overlapping their borders?

We need devote no more space to the projects of a projector – in the next generation the grandson of a deprived and plundered royalist clergyman, Dean Swift, would put paid to the type. 'Peters was not original in his suggestions. He gathered many of them from his own experiences and observations in Holland and America, and during his travels in England, Wales and Ireland. He acknowledges Bacon as the source of many of his scientific and technical suggestions.' Holland was the example to follow, not France as with the Stuarts, or Italy as with the Elizabethans. 'Though Holland seem to get the start of us, yet we may so follow as to stand at length upon their shoulders, and so see further.' There was patriotism in that, and at length this more or less came about.

Meanwhile, the Commonwealth was engaged in war with Holland, its fellow Protestant republic. Perhaps this was the beginning of disillusionment for Hugh, and it brought him even closer to Cromwell, who was also opposed to the war. As soon as he sent Parliament packing – which the King had been unable to do – and become Protector, he made peace with Holland. 'Peters' misgivings at the establishment of the Protectorate arose from doubts about the course of the Saints, rather than from any mistrust of Oliver Cromwell. The failures of the Rump and of the Barebone's Parliaments contrasted strongly with the long list of successes of the New Model Army ... Doubts occasionally assailed him, giving rise to an uneasiness of spirit which, because of ill health and continued public disorders and dissensions in the late 1650s, developed into an infinite sadness.' So too with Cromwell's final depression and disillusionment, his death-bed despair.

Cromwell's personal rule had an important job for his Congregational archbishop: Peters and Philip Nye became leading members of the Triers, the commissioners appointed to try and test every candidate for livings throughout the country. It was an onerous job: each candidate had to present three or more certificates of fitness from other ministers. Peters and Nye, both Independents, proceeded on the basis of Cromwell's idea of toleration: 'Though a man be of any of those three judgements [i.e. Presbyterian, Independent or Baptist], if he have the root of the matter in him, he may be admitted.' Professor Patrick concludes, 'like Peters, the Triers stressed moral qualifications, practically ignoring doctrinal ones; also like him, the Board was opportunistic and simple.' Most ministers in the countryside were, like sensible men, conformable enough – Hobbes would have approved; a good deal of variation prevailed, without a uniform system. Like Cromwell, and like Peters again, all was opportunist and pragmatic, making the best of circumstances as they were. There was nothing lasting about it – it would last only as long as Oliver Cromwell did and the rule of the Army. Before he died, his brother-in-law – the scientist Wilkins – told him that religion in England could be regulated only by bishops. In the end, the martyred Laud prevailed, not Peters. People agreed that the Triers administered their task – as Cromwell did his rule – conscientiously and ably enough.

In Cromwell's last year he found a use for Peters in the alliance with France to make war against Spain. He was sent to Dunkirk to preach to the army with something of his old enthusiasm. He set himself to convert the townsfolk, cheered the sick and wounded, and as of old meddled with everything. He even had interviews off his own bat with Cardinal Mazarin. The English ambassador reported, 'Mr Peters hath taken leave at least three or four times, but still something falls out which hinders his return to England. I must give him that testimony that he gave us three or four very honest sermons, and if it were possible to get him to mind preaching and to forbear the troubling of himself with other things, he would certainly prove a very fit minister for soldiers.'

On his return disillusionment set in. 'I am very much taken of my age and other ways from busy business, and would fain see Jesus.' On the collapse of Richard

Cromwell's Protectorate the Rump, with its Presbyterians, came back for a short space. An alarming pamphlet war was unleashed against Peters, and – without Oliver Cromwell – he had not a friend to defend him. When Monk came to London to bring about the Restoration, Peters was turned out of his quarters in Whitehall. On the King's return he went into hiding, as did the luckier Milton. Peters was ready to submit, but Presbyterians and Royalists at length had their revenge, and he was excepted from pardon. So were others, actual regicides who had signed the King's death warrant, but were not executed. Everyone saw a ready scapegoat in the notorious popular preacher.

Unearthed in Southwark, where he had taken refuge with a family of some obscure sect, he was confined in the Tower, where he wrote his last, best book: *A Dying Father's Last Legacy to an Only Child.* 'I wish I never had been vain in a vain world,' he said. It reminds one of Laud's words in the same place – how sick he was of the world and longing to leave it. Hugh warned his daughter to take heed of his own failings, warning her against 'that spreading evil of being a busybody, and pragmatical … Oh, keep home, keep home; I speak experience to you, who never found good hour but in mine own work. Nor do I take pleasure in remembering any my least activity in state matters … I am heartily sorry I was *popular*, and known better to others than myself.'

Indeed one wonders whether he had known himself all along, any more than Oliver Cromwell had. They were both borne up on the current of events, both highly temperamental, their temperaments up and down with events, manic-depressives with the demonic energy of manics. Evidently Peters had a glimpse of his true self in the Tower, and at the end came to terms with himself. We see this with his plea at his trial that 'his heart was right to God, and that he came into England, first, for religion;

secondly, for the law; thirdly, for the poor'. It was true enough that, in the mingled skein of our lives, he had done a great deal of good. The judge broke in to say coldly, 'Mr Peters, you are not questioned for any good you have done.'

No one had any doubt that he would be condemned, everyone was expecting him to show fear. He was to be hanged and disembowelled at Charing Cross, in sight of Whitehall where the King had stepped forth from the Banqueting Hall to his execution. Peters and his fellow, John Cook, were driven from Newgate – where Hugh had preached his last sermon – through the streets on hurdles, jeered at by the mob. Hugh was forced to watch the hanging and disembowelling of Cook, when the hangman came towards him, rubbing his bloody hands with, 'Come, how do you like this, Master Peters, how do you like this work?' Hugh answered, 'I am not, I thank God, terrified at it: you may do your worst.' After a silent prayer he said, 'This is a good day: he is come that I have long looked for, and I shall be with him in glory', and looked down on the crowd smiling.

The official news-sheet tells us how they reacted. 'There never was person suffered death so unpitied, and – which is more – whose execution was the delight of the people. Which they expressed by several shouts and acclamations, not only when they saw him go up the ladder and when the halter was putting about his neck; but also when his head was cut off, and held up aloft upon the end of a spear, there was such a shout as if the people of England had acquired a victory.'

It was perhaps an object-lesson not to be *popular*.

Sources: 'Peters' was the form of the name as generally used at the time, and also in Cornwall; it is a piece of pedantry to call him 'Peter', as does R.P. Stearns in his standard biography: *The Strenuous Puritan: Hugh Peter 1598-1660* (Univ. of Illinois Press, 1954). J. Max Patrick: *Hugh Peters, A Study in Puritanism* (Univ. of Buffalo Studies, 1946) deals more fully with Peters' writings and thinking. Most of my quotations come from these sources. Stearns' account of Peters' Cornish ancestry is inaccurate. See J.L. Vivian, *The Visitations of Cornwall*, and Mary Coate, *Cornwall in the Great Civil War*.

CHAPTER 5

John Selden and the Middle Way

I

Aubrey tells us that, when Hobbes's *Leviathan* came out, he sent a well-bound copy of it, by his stationer's man, to John Selden, the greatest scholar in the country. Selden did not know Hobbes, but returned a message that he would be very glad to be acquainted with him. Whereupon Hobbes waited upon him at his house in Whitefriars where he lived in considerable opulence – his collections of antiquities, marbles and inscriptions about him – and they maintained a strict friendship to Selden's dying day. It was in fact not far off: Selden died in 1654 and was given a splendid funeral in the Temple Church, where one sees his gravestone that survived the barbarous wreckage of the Germans in their Second War.

Aubrey knew Selden well, and describes his appearance for us. 'He was very tall, I guess about 6 foot high; sharp oval face; head not very big; long nose inclining to one side; full popping eye (grey)', (popping means full, protuberant). I possess a portrait that might be of him, which looks across the room at me as I write. Some later portraits give him long ringlets, but this portrait is of a severer Parliamentarian of about 1640, hair moderately long. The face agrees with other portraits, the full eyes, long nose and the rarer feature of a slightly cleft chin. He is a scholar, sober black garb and plain white collar; he has the favourite scholar's motto, *Magis amica veritas*, from the Latin tag that tells us, 'Plato is a friend, Aristotle is a friend, but a greater friend is truth.' The portrait, exceptionally for the time, bears no coat of arms, and Selden, a yeoman's son, had no arms. His mother, who came from a good Kentish family, had a coat, but Aubrey tells us, 'he had none of his own, though he so well deserved it. 'Tis strange, methinks, that he would not have one.'

He was regarded with immense respect on both sides, a difficult feat in that quarrelsome time; but, after all, he was not only its foremost jurist, whose opinion on legal precedents of all kinds was eagerly sought, but as an Orientalist, a leading authority on Jewish origins as well as the best Arabic scholar before Pococke. In addition, there was his work on Early English institutions and chronicles, as well as on classical sculpture and inscriptions. He was a dedicated scholar in many fields, passionately devoted to study, though in his prime he took an important part in public affairs. Nor has he been forgotten today: the Selden Society, which publishes so many valuable works and documents on legal history, keeps his memory green. Researchers in Duke Humphrey's Library, the ancient part of the Bodleian at Oxford, are familiar with Selden End, where his books were kept: he was a great benefactor.

He was an Oxford man, like Hobbes and Clarendon belonging to the institutions that emerged as Hertford College – the two former to Magdalen Hall, Selden to Hart Hall. He was born in a yeoman's thatched cottage, which remained up to the last century, in the parish of West Tarring, Sussex. Aubrey tells us how, in the good old times, his father took delight in playing on the violin and at Christmas time would play for his neighbours as they danced. One time at dinner at Sir Thomas Alford's during the Christmas holidays – which extended to Twelfth Night – 'Mr John Selden, then a young student sat at the lower end of the table, who was looked upon then to be of parts extraordinary and, somebody asking who he was, 'twas replied, "His son that is playing on the violin in the hall." ' Evidently the superior youth was dining with the gentry.

After a couple of years at little Clifford's Inn, at twenty he was admitted to Inner Temple, where 'his chamber was in Paper Buildings which look towards the garden'. Here he had an attic staircase with a tiny gallery to walk in. Though called to the bar in 1612, he did not practise much but was consulted on important cases which required special expertise. Learning was his passion; he could not have enough of it. In all his years in the Inner Temple he refused to take on offices, declining even to become Reader, and for this was fined and disabled from senior office, until his fame for learning made it impossible to discountenance him any further. Not until approaching fifty did he become a Bencher.

He was early taken notice of outside; in his twenties he became a member of the foremost literary and antiquarian circle in London, around Ben Jonson, Camden and Sir Robert Cotton, whose remarkable library with its many manuscripts and documents was made open to him. When Ben came out of prison for his part in *Eastward Ho* reflecting on the Scots, he banqueted his friends, Camden and Selden foremost among them. For the publication of *Volpone* the young lawyer wrote a prefatory poem, and 'a learned copy of verses' before Arthur Hopton's *A Concordancy of Years*, 1612. Already he was writing and publishing on early English history, an *Analecton* giving a summary of British history up to the Norman Conquest, and *England's Epinomia* tracing the laws and customs of the various peoples that constitute the mixed population of the island. When he provided the notes to the first eighteen books of Drayton's *Polyolbion*, one of the friends joked whether he had written on Drayton's poem, or Drayton written his poem on the basis of Selden's notes. A passion for antiquities was a keynote of the circle, and of this Selden became the 'Monarch in Letters' that Ben dubbed him.

The youthful William Browne's *Britannia's Pastorals* came out in 1613, for which Selden wrote prefatory verses in Greek, Latin and English:

> So much a stranger my severer Muse
> Is not to love-strains, or a shepherd's reed,
>   But that she knows some rites of Phoebus' dues,
> Of Pan, of Pallas, and her Sisters' meed.
> Read and commend she durst these tuned essays
> Of him that loves her. She hath ever found
> Her studies as one circle.

This gives us a clue to Selden: though a foremost authority in his special field of legal history and precedent, he was no narrow pedant yoked to one discipline. His insatiable curiosity led him into many fields, to all of which he made valuable contributions.

In 1614 he published his tall folio, *Titles of Honour*, dedicated to his chamber-fellow, or chum, Edward Heyward. This is an extraordinarily complete compilation of titles, from emperors, popes, kings downwards, their precedence and how to address them, treated with a vast knowledge of history, geography and diplomatic. Impossible as it is to read this constipated work, it had its utility when struggles for precedence between ambassadors of various monarchs caused a great deal of trouble, and frequently a fracas in the streets. In those days when there were no public libraries – except the unique Bodleian – Selden consulted books in Ben Jonson's well-stocked collection, which eventually came to include several of Selden's, presented, according to Ben's Latin inscription, by his 'dearest friend'.

5. John Selden and the Middle Way

Selden was now becoming, with his cumulative stores of learning, exceptionally prolific. In 1616 he edited Fortescue's classic on the Laws of England, and in 1617 no less than four works: two tracts on the Lord Chancellor's office and on the Jews in England, and two solid books. His *De Diis Syris*, on the Syrian gods, is the first of his Oriental studies; this brought him European fame, and it was reprinted, besides being made use of in other works, on the Continent. It was a pioneering venture in the field of mythology and comparative religion, and no doubt for Selden a formative influence in his scepticism with regard to the absolute claims of all religions. Naturally the book suffered from the exaggerated opinion of the time as to the antiquity of the Hebrew tongue (it was thought to have been the language of Eden, though one luminary thought that that was High German), and was vitiated by the traditional authority and chronology accorded to the books of the Bible.

The second book of that year was his classic *History of Tithes*, which brought Selden much notoriety and a rumpus. For tithes – paid on every kind of product from the land in every parish in the country for the upkeep of the Church and the clergy – were a bone of contention everywhere, a source of dissension threatening to become a national issue. Underlying the issue was whether they were levied by divine right, God's command, or were merely customary, of human invention. Selden was characteristically cagey about expressing himself on this burning topic, though what he thought was clear enough from his lawyer's veneration of the common law, as against ecclesiastical. 'The practised common law hath never given way herein to the canons [i.e. canon law], but hath allowed customs and made them subject to all civil titles.' As if the implication of that were not clear enough he pointed to the clerical opposition to the spread of knowledge which Renaissance humanists like Reuchlin, Budé and Erasmus had encountered. One sees his affiliations, critical, rational, sceptical.

The book provoked a storm, and Selden was carpeted before the Court of High Commission and made to apologise for his work. It is noticeable, however, that he said nothing with regard to the issue or the book's contents; he merely expressed regret at its publication, and it was suppressed – his most valuable and lasting contribution to learning. Nothing daunted, Selden pressed on and next produced an edition of the six books of Eadmer's Chronicle, from the manuscript in Sir Robert Cotton's library, giving an account of the first Norman kings after the Conquest. James I took favourable notice of the man becoming the first scholar in the kingdom, and thrice summoned him to know his opinion on the kind of thing that interested this theologically-minded monarch: what was actually the birthday of Jesus, what was the meaning of the notorious passage in *Revelation* concerning the number 666 (which has exercised so many feeble minds) and what should be thought of the sainted Calvin's explanation of this riveting subject?

A more useful commission from James I was a request for a tract on the English claim to dominion of the seas, in reply to the great Grotius' *Mare Liberum*. The Dutch had the largest merchant navy in Europe, with the smallest coast-line; so naturally they were in favour of the freedom of the seas, and their foremost legal scholar put the case for them in his classic work. Notwithstanding, because Grotius was an opponent of the popular Calvinist party, he was condemned to life imprisonment, escaping after three years – appropriately in a box of books – to freedom abroad and to think as he liked. On the real question of maritime rights English interests, with far longer coasts and smaller merchant fleets, were opposed to the Dutch. Selden was called in to argue the English case, which ultimately emerged as his *Mare Clausum*, immensely popular with both King and Parliament.

James I and the House of Commons were already in dispute as to its rights; as Selden was a lawyer, he venerated the common law, as they all did, and was consulted by the Commons as to precedents, before even he became a member. The King took umbrage at Selden's support of the Commons' Protestation of its rights; he and some others were briefly committed to the custody of the sheriff of London. A few months later even Lord Chancellor Bacon was consulting him as to the validity of the Lords' judgments when it wasn't clear whether the House was in regular session or merely convened. We have a letter of Selden on this subject, full of the barely intelligible argy-bargy lawyers delighted in. However, it was generally noticed that Selden spoke more clearly and concisely than he wrote – a reason why his *Table Talk* is so much more readable than any of his books.

Charles I's Parliaments, from 1625 to 1629, witnessed a growing breach between King and a House of Commons becoming ever more dissatisfied with the conduct of the nation's affairs, increasingly aggressive and demanding a share in it. This was understandable, for the policies of the two young men, Charles and Buckingham, were as haphazard as administration was inefficient. Partly out of resentment at the failure to secure a Spanish marriage – after the absurd venture of their journey to Madrid – and also to curry favour with popular anti-Spanish feeling, they involved themselves in a war with Spain. It was ill-conducted, and an expedition to Cadiz failed – a marked contrast with the Elizabethan capture of the city, of which Essex had garnered all the renown. (His son went into opposition and became the Parliamentary general at the beginning of the Civil War.)

The two young men also embarked on a war with France – with inconceivable foolishness when they could have had an alliance with France, which was hostile to Spain. France and Spain came to terms instead, leaving Charles and Buckingham again to seek popularity by expeditions to relieve Protestant La Rochelle. These were expensive failures, and with governments nothing fails like failure. Charles and Buckingham persisted. The wars needed money; Parliament demanded inquiry into how it was spent, and into the inefficiency of Buckingham's administration. This raised other issues, and increasingly the spectre of the Crown's ministers being made responsible to Parliament. This was new ground, an invasion of the prerogative – in it the issue of the Civil War was foreshadowed; and, what proved fatal in the long run, it produced an ominous breach of confidence between King and Parliament, or, we may say, with the gentry and middle classes at large, the backbone of the nation.

Such was the background of Selden's Parliamentary career in these years. Though not a politician in the first place, he was prominent in debates, in which he aligned himself with the opposition. It is surprising that so reflective a man was prepared to support the Parliamentary firebrand, Sir John Eliot, with his intemperate oratory. But the one passion in Selden's unimpassioned nature was for the liberty of the subject, liberty to think for himself: when this was threatened, he spoke up. In these early years the threat to liberty came from the executive; so Selden took sides with the opposition. We shall see how he behaved later, when the threat came from the other side and revolution took over.

As the most eminent jurist of the day Selden was regularly consulted as to the legal issues involved. In the Parliament of 1626 he supported the demand for Buckingham's impeachment, the only way in which Parliament could bring home to him his responsibility for the government's failures. The legal question was whether the House of Commons could institute proceedings as such, when no individual had raised a charge against the minister. Selden provided the argument in favour of impeachment – 'Else no great man shall, for fear of danger, be accused by any particular man.' We see the bluntness of the constitutional instruments in this rather primitive stage of their development: attainder – such as was later applied against Strafford and Laud – was even clumsier: murder by act of Parliament. Responsibility of the executive to Parliament was long in being worked out, via civil war and revolution – men so hardly realise 'what a little foolery governs the whole world', Selden was to say, later.

In the absence of Parliamentary grants to carry on the wars, government was reduced to the expedient of a forced loan. This met with resistance from gentry all over the country, and some were committed to prison by the Privy Council for their refusal. This produced the Five Knights' case, who demanded a *habeas corpus*. The legal point was this: no one denied that King and Council had a right to imprison, but the defendants argued that cause of imprisonment must be given so that the case might be tried at common law. Here we see the conflict between common law and the prerogative, which was to lead to the abolition of the prerogative courts later in 1641 – in which Selden was to take a hand. In the Five Knights' case of 1627 Selden appeared to defend Sir Edmund Hampden – a name of ill-omen for Charles I later. Selden's argument pushed forward into new ground, for upon it King and Privy Council 'would be reduced to the position occupied in less important cases by ordinary justices of the peace'.[1] Once more the Commons' battle was fought by the exponents of the common law – hardly surprising since both were institutions, and weapons, of the ruling gentry, rather than the people at large.

[1] S.R. Gardiner, *History of England* (ed. 1904), VI.214.

For the opening of Parliament in March 1628 Laud preached on the text, 'Endeavour to keep the unity of the Spirit in the bond of peace.' Conflict continued, but Coke, Wentworth and Selden agreed that the rights of subjects must be vindicated before grants of money were made. They opposed the billeting of soldiers, impressing men for the army, the resort to martial law. Debates raged to and fro, solid arguments mixed with a great deal of humbug as usual, and disagreements with the Lords. An unimpressive peer, the Earl of Suffolk – whose father had built Audley End out of embezzlement from the Treasury and whose sister had had Sir Thomas Overbury poisoned in the Tower – charged Selden with erasing a record. 'Will you not hang Selden? He deserves to be hanged.' The charge was untrue, and the miserable peer denied his words.

The constitutional struggle broadened; the Commons put forward a summary of the subjects' liberties, which they demanded that the King should observe, in the Petition of Right. This came to be regarded as a landmark in constitutional history: no taxes or forced loans without consent of Parliament, limitation upon billeting and martial law, death sentence to be by the laws and statutes of the realm, no imprisonment without cause given, etc. Ominously, Magna Carta was cited. It fell to Selden to bring in the historic document before Parliament. To make it palatable to the King a large grant of five subsidies was made, conditional upon it. The King signed up, on the understanding that the Petition did no more than state rights such as previously existed.

Charles I, however, refused to give up Buckingham, whose conduct of war and policy continued with as ill success as before. In June Selden proposed to take up his impeachment again. The King headed this off by proroguing Parliament. In the opening session of January 1629 Selden took the lead in bringing up two cases in which liberty of the subject had been attacked. One Savage 'had lately lost his ears by a decree of Star Chamber, by an arbitrary judgment … Next they will take away our arms, and then our legs, and so our lives. Customs creep on us …'[2] This was outspoken for him; he complained that the Petition of Right had been violated.

Religion was as much a bone of contention as constitutional liberties. The temper of the Commons was Protestant, part Puritan: no sympathy for the civilised anti-Calvinism of Charles and Laud with their devotion to 'the beauty of holiness', the reparation of some of the damage done by the Reformation. Just as Selden was a consistent upholder of individual liberty, so he was a consistent Erastian, holding no brief for clerics of either party forcing their views upon people. He held that the state would hold the ring more fairly than sectarian dogmatists. The Commons took offence at the proceedings and utterances of High Church bishops and divines – in fact, it would have been expedient to lower them a little in a hotly Protestant country. A resolution was passed affirming the Protestant sense of the Thirty-Nine Articles, and rejecting 'the sense of the Jesuits and Arminians', i.e. High Churchmen. Selden wished to add that the Articles derived their authority from Parliament, not from Convocation.

He was ahead of contemporary opinion on the subject of the licensing of books; some control was necessary, and it was tolerantly exercised through the Church authorities, deputies for the Archbishop of Canterbury and Bishop of London. The Commonwealth later found it necessary to exercise some censorship, and called in that prime exponent of liberty of thought, John Milton, to execute it. When the question came up, Selden surprised the Commons with a very libertarian view. 'There is no law to prevent the printing of any book in England, but only a

---

[2] Ibid., VII.31.

decree in Star Chamber. Therefore that a man should be fined, imprisoned, and his goods taken from him, is a great invasion of the liberty of the subject. I desire, therefore, that a law may be made on this.'[3] Too delicate a subject to touch, nothing was done about it. (In our enlightened age the issue re-appears in regard to popular pornography.)

The just-minded, if somewhat naif, historian Gardiner sums up on this: 'Selden's unenthusiastic nature and wide learning had made him utterly indifferent to the theological disputes with which the air resounded, and he thought it very hard that anyone should suffer because he held one view or another on a speculative question. He was no more born to be a martyr of liberty than a martyr of orthodoxy ... On the whole, he attached himself to the popular party. But his object was not to seize upon power in order that it might be turned against those who held it. Power itself, he held, needed to be diminished.' Gardiner continues in a sense not very partial to Selden, referring to his 'indifference to the issues which seemed so momentous'. This judgment seems hardly fair when Selden had been imprisoned for the outright expression of his views. Where liberty was concerned he was by no means 'indifferent'.

To this there was one exception. The Roman Church, wherever it ruled, was not libertarian: its claims were totalitarian. It was a bad liability for Charles I that his Queen was a Catholic, still more that she was an indefatigable proselytiser, always pressing her entourage to vert to Catholicism. Under her protection and in her vicinity Catholics increased; this was a further liability to Charles whose support of Laud was already resented by Parliament. Laud engaged in an ecumenical dialogue with Rome, one would have supposed a good Christian proceeding; he was in fact a firm Anglican, but was always hounded as a 'Papist' by Puritans. He wished to keep the

[3] Ibid., VII.50-1.

balance even by discouraging Papists and Puritans alike. But when a Jesuit seminary was uncovered at Clerkenwell, the ten priests brought into the light of day were reprieved by the King's order, contrary to the law. Selden took this up in Parliament and made an issue of it – and this affords a contrast with his later attitude.

A more complex issue arose over the question of tonnage and poundage, the customs duties which had regularly been granted to the Crown at the beginning of every reign. 'The attempt of the House of Commons to convert this formal consent into a right of refusal must have seemed to [the King] an unwarrantable shifting of the balance of the constitution.'[4] It was indeed an intrusion into the sphere of the prerogative, and Selden went out on a limb in supporting Eliot in challenging it. Even Gardiner – too favourably inclined, as a Victorian, to Parliamentary rhetoric – condemns Eliot for making compromise impossible. 'He could not see that he was striking away all the supports of the royal authority ... and whether his course was to be justified by precedents and reason or not, it was one to which no sovereign with the slightest feeling of self-respect was likely to submit.' Eliot was making it impossible to carry on the King's government; the surprising thing is that Selden should have aided and abetted him, against the better judgment of Pym.

'Once more,' Gardiner judges, 'Selden failed to rise to the height of the argument: if a point of privilege was raised, he said, all other matters must give place.'[5] In other words, Selden was no statesman any more than Eliot was: one was a doctrinaire jurist, the other a demagogue, as the King regarded him. An open collision ensued: 'of the leaders who had stood by Eliot's side in the great struggle for the Petition of Right, Selden alone supported him now.' The

[4] Ibid., 58-9.
[5] Ibid., 62, 67, 76.

King sent a message adjourning Parliament. The Speaker tried to obey and leave the chair. Selden proposed, quite unconstitutionally, that Eliot should take the Speaker's place and appeal to the country. There followed the notorious episode when the Speaker was held down in the chair, while the resolutions against both the King's ecclesiastical policy and his rights regarding the customs revenue were put. Then the House adjourned itself. The King dissolved it. 'Eleven years were to pass away before the representatives of the country were permitted to cross that threshold again.'

It remained to bring those responsible for the breach to book: it was unconstitutional to resist the King's order to adjourn, an open flouting of authority. The leaders in this were imprisoned, Eliot and Selden sent to the Tower. Examined before the Council, Eliot refused to answer any question relating to anything done in the House of Commons. In this stand he remained obstinate, dying eventually in the Tower, a martyr to liberty – and consumption. Selden was not of the stuff of which martyrs are made – fortunately, or we should have missed many good works to come. He denied his part in the fateful day's proceedings, and explained his motion as an attempt to help on the adjournment of the House in accord with the King's message. 'He could never for an instant have expected to be believed,' comments the Victorian moralist; 'all he meant was to intimate that he had no intention of allowing himself to be made a victim for any opinion whatever.'[6] By not becoming a martyr Selden had many good services yet to perform: the best were still to come.

Parliament had been dissolved in March. In May the imprisoned members – all except the uncompromising Eliot – applied for writs of *habeas corpus*, for which Selden supplied the argument. This was that their proceedings

---

[6] Ibid., 80.

were covered by privilege of Parliament, and not within the purview of Star Chamber. He also supplied arguments that gave the government some difficulty regarding bail for the imprisoned MPs. At first he was denied books and papers, a very real deprivation for one who depended on them – being in the Tower was in itself no dishonour. Charles was inclined to treat the eminent jurist leniently, though he did not permit bail. Shortly, Selden was removed from the Tower to the Marshalsea, and subsequently the Gatehouse at Westminster, where he had more liberty to receive his friends and continue his studies, free from the distractions of Parliament.

It was not until May 1631 that he was liberated, when the Earls of Arundel and Pembroke pleaded that they needed his special knowledge in litigation upon which they were engaged. Even so he had to give security for appearance in court for the next three years. With Parliament in abeyance, under the King's personal rule as under Elizabeth I, peace settled upon the land.

II

The suspending of Parliament for more than a decade marked an epoch, and gave many people second thoughts – almost certainly Selden among them, though he does not give himself away and there is no hint of it in his papers. But those angry proceedings in which he had been involved cannot but have had an effect upon his mind, as upon others. Wentworth, who had been opposed to Buckingham, became a foremost minister in the King's service (though sabotaged, like Laud, by the feckless French Queen) – at first kept in the North, and then in Ireland. Weston brought order into the Crown's financial affairs, on a basis which fortunately restricted an active foreign policy: while Europe exhausted itself in the Thirty Years' War, England enjoyed peace. Laud continued to rule the Church, and to take an increasing part in the state – to the fury of Puritans, thousands of whom left the country to set so blissful a model of toleration in New England.

Meanwhile, Selden's private and scholarly life pursued its prosperous course; nothing distracted him from research and writing. His devotion to the principle of liberty did not mean that he had any democratic illusions. 'So generous, so ingenuous, so proportioned to good, such fosterers of virtue, so industrious – of such mould are the few. So inhuman, so blind, so dissembling, so vain, so justly nothing but what's ill disposition – are the most.' His tastes were those of the elect, and he was already a connoisseur and collector of antiquities and curios, coins and marbles. In 1624 he had published his account of the marbles and ancient sculptures which the magnificent Earl of Arundel had brought home from Italy, with their inscriptions: *Marmora Arundelliana*, which was reprinted like most of his books, abroad as well as at home.

In 1631 he published the first of his investigations into Hebrew antiquity, on the succession to property and goods in ancient Jewish law. This was followed by works at intervals on the succession of religious leaders among the Jews (this dedicated to Laud); on natural law according to the Hebrew dispensation; on marriage and divorce among the ancient Jews; and on the Jewish Sanhedrim, a work in three parts he did not live to finish. Until the prime of Pococke, Selden was the leading Hebrew scholar among the English, well equipped in Arabic too. At much trouble and expense Archbishop Laud was collecting the Oriental manuscripts for Oxford, which made it the leading centre for such learning for a century; and Pococke was Laud's *protégé*. An excellent scholar himself, the Archbishop was anxious to advance scholarship; these interests brought him and Selden together, and they became friends: 'both a frequent and a welcome guest at Lambeth House, where he was grown into such esteem with the Archbishop that he might have chosen his own preferment in the Court, had he not undervalued all other employments in respect of his studies.'

Perhaps Laud wished to win him over to the side of the King – it would have been a notable victory. No bad blood seems to have subsisted between the King and Selden, who took part in organising a splendid masque given by the Inns of Court on Charles's return from his coronation in Scotland. Intended as an expression of their loyalty, it was also a riposte to the attack on plays and masques, *Histriomastix*, with its insinuations against the Queen, by their fellow-barrister, the intolerable Prynne. Puritans hated the theatre. A letter from Selden to Ben Jonson interprets for him the passage in *Deuteronomy* which Puritans took to mean God's veto upon an actor wearing female dress. This was particularly repugnant to Puritan virtue – and one sees the awkward approaches it might lead to from the Induction to *The Taming of a Shrew*.

Selden was one of the few men for whom Jonson had no word of criticism: he told Drummond that Selden is 'the law-book of the judges of England, the bravest [foremost] man in all languages'. The doyen of literary life addressed an Epistle to the acknowledged master in legal lore:

Stand forth my object, then, you that have been
Ever at home, yet have all countries seen;
And, like a compass, keeping one foot still
Upon your centre, do your circle fill
Of general knowledge; watched men, manners too,
Heard what times past have said, seen what ours do ...
What fables have you vexed! what truth redeemed!
Antiquities searched! Opinions disesteemed!
Impostures branded, and authorities urged!
What blots and errors have you watched and purged
Records and authors of! how rectified
Times, manners, customs! Innovations spied ...

A consequence of Selden's acquaintance with Laud was a royal command, a mark of approbation, that he should take up his work again on the English claim to dominion of the seas around the coasts of the British Isles. Thus appeared his celebrated *Mare Clausum* in 1636. Charles was so pleased with it that he directed an official copy be kept by the Privy Council, another in the Exchequer, and a third in the Court of Admiralty.

Selden's personal life was bound up with the family of the Earl of Kent, particularly with the Countess, an intelligent woman, grand-daughter of Bess of Hardwick. He acted as their solicitor and steward, though the connexion may have been closer. Aubrey says that, after the Earl's death in 1639, Selden married the Countess; there is no open evidence of this, but he may well have consoled the widow. She had literary interests and wrote a book or two, about physic and cooking. Certainly Selden was in clover with her, in the country at Wrest Park in Bedfordshire, in London at the Friary house in Whitefriars, 'which was, before the conflagration, a noble dwelling. He never kept any servant peculiar, but my lady's were all at his command.' He speaks proprietorily of the mansion as '*museum meum Carmeliticum*', and there about him was his splendid library, his cabinets and cases, his Chinese map and his marbles. The Countess died some three years before him, leaving him all her personal property. Aubrey says that 'he never owned the marriage with the Countess of Kent till after her death, upon some law account'. That may well have meant some restriction upon her jointure, and sounds plausible.

Thus the 'halcyon' years of the 1630s passed – which were so affectingly described by Clarendon – before the storm broke in the North. Charles and Laud never imagined that the Scots would be so unreasonable as to unleash a national rebellion over an improved service-book.

5. John Selden and the Middle Way

The fiasco of the two Border confrontations necessitated the calling of Parliament, for the Scots would not go away without a large payment in cash. Henceforth the collusion between Presbyterian Scots and the English Parliament to end Charles I's personal rule, for government on Parliament's conditions in Church and state.

Selden was returned to the Long Parliament in 1640 for the university of Oxford and, after the death of his colleague, remained as its sole representative – rather oddly, a Parliament man, when the sympathies of the university were with the King. As was to be expected, he took a line of his own, but one notices his moderation – also in keeping with his idea of justice – in struggling hard in committee against Strafford's attainder. Nor was he in favour of backing the petition of the London Puritans, rigged as it was, against episcopacy. Selden remained consistently Erastian, in favour of running the Church by bishops but under lay control: no divine right nonsense. He was equally consistent in promoting action against the prerogative courts, himself leading the attack on the court of the Marshal and bringing in bills declaring Ship-money illegal, restricting the royal forests and their jurisdiction, and abolishing fines on taking up forced knighthood.

Virtual unity in the Commons prevailed in ending the King's personal rule; the breach came with the attack on the established Church and the clear intention of the majority to attack the constitutional rights of the Crown. This gave the King a party; Falkland and Hyde, good Parliamentarians, moved over into his service. Lord Keeper Littleton was not much good in his job, and depended for advice on Selden, 'with whom he had great friendship'. Charles took the seals from Littleton, but the next in succession, Lord Chief Justice Bankes, was afraid to take on the job in circumstances threatening war. The King, who had withdrawn to York, thought of Selden, but Falkland and Hyde were certain that he would refuse office: 'he was in years and of a tender constitution; he had for many years enjoyed his ease, which he loved, and would not have made a journey to York or have lain out of his own bed for any preferment, which he had never affected.'

Civil war threatened. The great majority of the nation wished for peace – and, as Hobbes said, were not concerned in the struggle within the governing class, but their wishes did not count in the naked struggle for power. Among the Parliamentarians at Westminster the peace party was headed by Holles and the lawyers, Selden, Whitelocke and Maynard. When the King issued his commissions of array to recruit armed men, Selden spoke out in the House against them as illegal, to the enthusiasm of the audience. When he similarly condemned the militia ordinances of the Commons, he was heard with great disfavour. With war on the way, there was no room for one who was against it; circumstances forced him to remain with Parliament – probably the balance of his convictions too, along with his Parliamentary past. Nor was there place for such a man, elderly and independent, in an active revolutionary government.

An appropriate, indeed an inevitable, posting for him was as a lay-member of the Westminster Assembly of divines, overwhelmingly Presbyterian, gathered to work out a confession of faith and an alternative structure in place of the traditional established Church. In this solemn assembly Selden was often in a minority of one; but, provocative as his stance was, he could not but be heard, for he was the best scholar on the Biblical texts they regarded as gospel truth, without always knowing their meaning. Selden was able to tell them, often confusing and annoying the elect. Whitelocke reports that 'Mr Selden spake admirably, and confuted divers of them in their own learning. Sometimes when they had a text of Scripture to prove their assertion, he would tell them, "Perhaps in your little pocket Bibles with gilt leaves the translation may be thus, but the Greek or the Hebrew signifies thus and thus", and so would totally silence them.'

This did not prevent these choice divines, who had outed the bishops for claiming divine right, from claiming it for themselves. He took advantage of his position in Parliament – on whose authority after all the Assembly sat – to draft articles which betrayed the exorbitance of their claims. Did the Assembly mean to imply that parochial and congregational elderships appointed by Parliament were of divine right? There followed a string of such questions, requesting that the answers be fortified by Scriptural proofs. He evidently enjoyed provoking the wiseacres. Fuller concluded that his aim was to perplex rather than to inform them, and rather to 'humble the juredivinoship of presbytery'. Sometimes he was able to reduce the proceedings to the level they merited, as when a dispute blew up as to the exact distance between Bethlehem and Jerusalem, calculated from the staying power of fish transported from one to the other: Selden confused the disputants by suggesting that perhaps the fish were salted.

In Parliament he was in a position to oppose the Assembly's petition that in every presbytery the pastors and elders should have the power of excommunication and of suspending from the sacrament. Here Selden was with the majority: Parliament had not ended episcopacy 'Root and Branch' in order to place the nation under the yoke of a lot of self-righteous Presbyterians. Even stiff-necked Milton was learning from experience that

New Presbyter is but old Priest writ large.

Parliament was determined to assert lay-control. However on the question of toleration Selden was in a small minority. Parliamentary toleration meant the exclusion of Anglicanism and the Church of Rome, i.e. the great majority of the nation. When Selden, advancing from his earlier position, moved in favour of toleration for Catholics as Christians, he was supported only by the unbelieving Henry Marten. To the Puritan mind Catholics were 'idolaters'; he answered by drawing the distinction between idolatry and prayer for the intercession of the saints. In vain, of course.

The shameful war drew to an end with victory for a minority Parliament dependent on its Army; and, after a second outbreak of war, the Army determined to hold the King responsible. A Declaration of his misdeeds was drawn up by the Rump of a Parliament, now under the control of the Army, in 1648. In this Declaration was a shocking charge of Charles's connivance in the 'murder' of his father – a charge which Milton twice lyingly repeated. Selden moved for the omission of the disgraceful charge – he had been on the committee which investigated the matter and found no cause for reflection on the King. Cromwell, who had now made up his mind, asked for Selden's expulsion from the House. Thus the whirligig of Time brings in its revenges.

With the 'trial' and execution of the King, Selden, like most of the best people in the country, withdrew from any further part in public affairs. In time of revolution, regicide and public murder, 'the wisest way for men is to say nothing'.

His position in Parliament had enabled him to render services to the universities and learning in this revolting time. During some years he was responsible for the keeping of the records in the Tower, sequestered into his hands. He saw to it that Archbishop Bancroft's confiscated library went to his university of Cambridge. Selden took a hand in forwarding Laud's precious Oriental manuscripts to the Bodleian at Oxford, for which his own library was intended. He managed to secure the recovery of Laud's endowment of the professorship of Arabic, and in 1647 he rendered good service by becoming one of the Parliamentary Visitors of the university. He took an active part in numerous sittings, in spite of age and poor health, to mitigate the damage done to his *alma mater*.

After the King's execution what was to become of his collections of books, antiquities, sculpture and paintings? The Commonwealth sold most of his pictures – the heaviest artistic loss this country has ever suffered, for Charles I was the finest and most discriminating collector the country ever had. He had kept his library in St James's Palace. In the summer after his execution Selden urged Whitelocke to undertake the keepership: 'if he did not undertake the charge, all those rare monuments of antiquity would be lost, and there were not the like to them – except in the Vatican – in any library in Christendom.' And in that time of depredation Selden preserved Sir Robert Cotton's library, to which he had the key.

Work is the only anodyne in evil times, and Selden continued his studies and to produce. He went on combining his work on ancient Jewish institutions with his earliest enthusiasm for English antiquities and chronicles. In 1647 he had produced an edition of *Fleta*, a thirteenth-century Latin text-book of English law; in 1652 he wrote accounts of the early medieval chroniclers for a collection that appeared as *Decem Scriptores*. In his last year he wrote, in Latin, a Vindication of his treatise on Dominion of the Seas against a Dutch jurist who imputed unworthy motives to him in writing it. Selden was angry at the imputation: I suspect patriotism was enough.

In November 1654 – the Commonwealth at an end and Cromwell monarchically installed as Lord Protector – Selden wrote a last letter to his old friend Whitelocke, asking urgently to see him: 'thus much wearies the most weak hand and body of your lordship's most humble servant.'[7] Apparently some question about his will troubled

[7] G.W. Johnson, *Memoirs of John Selden*, 349.

him. His old barber – whom Selden used to irritate by interrupting his ministrations to jot down a note of an idea (just like Bacon and Hobbes) – said, 'I never knew a wise man make a wise will.' Selden left a large estate, some £40,000 – the Countess must doubtless have been his wife and left him everything. He was not going to leave it uselessly to his lower-class relations: 'I have no one to make my heir, except a milkmaid; and such people do not know what to do with a great estate.' He made two eminent lawyers and two others his executors, and they made the best disposal of his possessions.

He had intended his fine library to go to the Bodleian; when he had been refused the loan of a manuscript, he changed his mind. After some negotiations with the Inner Temple, the executors made the right disposition and sent the 8,000 volumes down to Oxford. So also with Selden's own collection of marbles: John Evelyn saw them there in 1669 well disposed around Archbishop Sheldon's new Theatre. Idiots were already beginning to scratch them: they had to be taken indoors for protection.

Selden died on 30 November 1654, within some days of attaining his seventieth year. He was given a grand send-off, 'all the Parliament men, all the Benchers and great officers; all the judges had mourning, as also abundance of people of quality.' Archbishop Usher, most learned of prelates, already old and frail, roused himself to preach the panegyric. Selden's generosity was recalled – how he had helped Dr Casaubon with a considerable sum in time of need; his aid to the publication of learned works, Walton's Polyglot Bible, Kelly's antiquarian travels, to other antiquarians, Ashmole and Farington, his help to young Hale whose quality he detected.

Aubrey, as usual, gives us endearing glimpses of his habits to bring him alive for us – how he would mock the Assembly of divines with 'I do consider the original', and was 'like a thorn in their sides, for he did baffle and vex them, and was able to run them all down with his Greek and antiquities ... He never used any artificial help to strengthen his memory: 'twas purely natural ... I have heard some divines say (I know not if maliciously) that 'twas true he was a man of great reading, but gave not his own sentiment.' We have seen that, as with Hobbes, in so precarious a time one could not say out loud all that one thought. 'In his younger years he affected obscurity of style which, after, he quite left off and wrote perspicuously. 'Twill be granted that he was one of the greatest critics of his time.'

As to his way of life: ' he kept a plentiful table, and was never without learned company. He was temperate in eating and drinking. He had a slight stuff or silk kind of false carpet to cast over the table where he read and his papers lay, when a stranger came in, so that he needed not to displace his books or papers' (a practice I have found it useful to adopt). Selden had a wide circle of friends, particularly among the lawyers. Among his younger acquaintance was little Mr Pepys, naturally enough, for their common interest in maritime matters.

Pepys had often heard the great jurist say that Henry VII expected Danish ships to strike sail to English even in the Baltic. On 29 November 1661 we find Pepys 'calling at Paul's Churchyard for a *Mare Clausum*, having it in my mind to write a little matter about the business of striking sail, and present it to the Duke [of York], which I now think will be a good way to make myself known'. On December 17th he sat late at the office 'and so home to supper and to Selden, *Mare Clausum*, and so to bed'. So also for several nights, 'sat late up reading of Mr Selden'; on Sunday, 22 December, 'went up to read in Mr Selden till church time'; and thus to 8 January, 'and so up to my study and read the two treaties before Mr Selden's *Mare Clausum*, and so to bed.' In 1663 Milton's All Souls protégé, Marchamont Needham, translated the work into English; on 21 April, 'up betimes and to my office, where first I ruled with red ink my English *Mare Clausum* which, with the new orthodox title, makes it now very handsome.' A few years later, 22 November 1667, 'to the Temple, and there walked a good while in the Temple church, observing the plainness of Selden's tomb, and how much better one of his executors hath, who is buried by him.' This was Selden's friend and executor, Vaughan, a Lord Chief Justice – and so the world opines, though who remembers Vaughan now?

III

Nevertheless, for all these helps, we should not have been able to see very far into this great scholar's mind if he had not had the luck to have a Boswell, to take down the words that fell from his lips in conversation. Selden's writings were rather impersonal and do not betray the inner man, while his public utterances were apt to be discreet – except for the flare-up in the Parliament of 1629. It is from his *Table Talk* that we can trace the impact of these events upon his mind, the conclusions he drew, the increasing moderation, the scepticism they generated in him – and no wonder! Selden's *Table Talk* offers as incisive a commentary as Hobbes's *Behemoth* on the time of civil war and revolution they both lived through, and they corroborate each other.

Selden's Boswell was his amanuensis, Richard Milward, and it was not until the freer atmosphere after the Revolution of 1688 that Selden's very free and *désabusé* mind could be revealed in the world. People who did not like it took refuge in the usual way of the obtuse in shutting their eyes, denying its authenticity – though it was as usual the third-rate who did so. A mind on a level with Selden's, Dr Johnson, for all his difference of opinion, knew better. One day, when Boswell was praising French memoirs of the kind, Dr Johnson said: 'a few of them are good, but we have one book of that kind better than any of them – Selden's *Table Talk*.' It is indeed a classic, by which he yet lives.

Its interest is mainly intellectual, in its general reflexions on society, politics, psychology, religion; but it offers some comments on the events of the time, which are helpful to the historian in judging them. Selden's evidence is singularly detached. He tells us that 'the bishops were too hasty, else with a discreet slowness they might have had what they aimed at'. It is true that Laud was tactless, an elderly man in a hurry: he had arrived at leadership in the Church too late to repair the damage that had been done by Abbot's long and supine primacy. If only Bancroft had lived to carry on his good work! Again, it might have been better if Laud had remained Bishop of London, and a more accommodating man been made Primate. On the other hand, he was right about the Lecturers pushed forward by the Puritan gentry: 'if there had been no Lecturers, which succeed the Friars in their way, the Church of England might have stood and flourished at this day ... Lecturers get a great deal of money, because they preach the people tame, as a man watches a hawk; and then they do what they list with them.' As for the people, when the Bible comes 'among the Common People, Lord, what gear they do make of it!'

As for preaching: 'preaching, for the most part, is the glory of the preacher, to show himself a fine man. Catechising would do much better.' This was what Elizabeth I thought, and no doubt Laud, who was Elizabethan in outlook. 'Preaching by the Spirit, as they call it, is most esteemed by the Common People, because they cannot abide art or learning, which they have not been bred up in.' As to the content of their preachments, 'when the preacher says "This is the meaning of the Holy Ghost" in such a place, in sense he can mean no more than this – that is, I, by studying the place, think this the meaning of the Holy Ghost.' This deflationary thought would have cut through a lot of nonsense, if only people had the sense to apply it. It is revealing to place what people 'think' as a numerator over the denominator of what makes them think it: the relationship to their motives or interest is usually obvious. It saves a great deal of time, for then one does not need to take seriously what people suppose themselves to think: few know how to *think*, properly speaking.

Preachers, both Selden and Hobbes thought, were responsible for much of the trouble at the time, particularly the Presbyterians. 'Presbyters have the greatest power of any clergy in the world, and gull the laity most.' His tactics in the Westminster Assembly are corroborated from his *Table Talk*: 'when the Queries [Articles, as above] were sent to the Assembly concerning the *Jus Divinum* [divine right] of Presbytery, their asking time to answer them was a satire upon themselves; for if it were to be seen in the text, they might quickly turn to the place and show us it. Their delaying to answer makes us think there's no such thing there.'

'The clergy would have us believe them against our own reason ... Chain up the clergy on both sides.' On the other hand, he could be fair in regard to the bishops who were blamed for punishing the lying libellers, Prynne and company. 'Men cry out upon the High Commission, as if the clergymen only had to do in it; when I believe there are more laymen in Commission there than clergymen. The people think the bishops only censured Prynne, Burton and Bastwick, when there were but two there, and one spake not in his own cause.' The people, who will believe anything, were taken in by Puritan propaganda and semantics. Similarly with their lies against Anglicans as Papists: 'we charge the prelatical clergy with Popery to make them odious, though we know they are guilty of no such thing.' Puritan propaganda was venomous and most effective: there was no effective defence against it.

152

5. John Selden and the Middle Way

Who, after all, is a heretic? ' 'Tis a vain thing to talk of a heretic, for a man for his heart can think no otherwise than he does think.' A mere matter of opinion: 'I love apples best of any fruit; it does not follow I must think apples to be the best fruit. Opinion is something wherein I go about to give reason why all the world should think as I think.' What gives man all the trouble, 'and made all the confusion in the world – that is Opinion.' And what nonsensical opinions people quarrel about: 'Predestination', for instance, 'is a point inaccessible, out of our reach; we can make no notion of it, 'tis so full of intricacy, so full of contradiction', i.e. evidently nonsense. People simply contradicted themselves in what they put forward: 'the Puritans will allow no free will at all, but God does all; yet will allow the subject his liberty to do or not to do. The Arminians, who hold we have free will, yet say, when we come to the king there must be all obedience, and no liberty.' Both merely want their own way: what they put forward is merely a smoke-screen for that. Who is taken in? Not Selden, or Hobbes.

Ordinary people are unaware of their own motives – this is what shocks those who know. The vociferous will preach against what they cannot make use of themselves, and 'get esteem by seeming to contemn them. But yet, mark it while you live, if they do not please themselves as much as they can; and we live more by example than precept.' 'You say there must be no human invention in the Church, nothing but the pure Word. *Answer*: If I give any exposition but what is in the text, that is my invention; if you give another exposition, that is your invention, and both are human.' Similarly with the appeal to Providence: 'we single out particulars [i.e. circumstances], and apply God's Providence to them. Thus when two are married and have undone one another, they cry it was God's Providence we should come together, when God's Providence does equally concur to everything.' Puritans, especially Oliver Cromwell, regularly appealed to their run of successes in the Civil War –

153

Marston Moor, Naseby, Dunbar, Worcester, Cromwell's 'crowning mercy' – as evidence that Providence was with them. 'Look at circumstantials,' he said, 'they hang so together.' Then what about 1660, when it was all reversed? Providence was merely a reflexion of men's ego writ large.

We have arrived at the modern scepticism of a Pareto. 'The Puritan would be judged by the Word of God: if he would speak clearly he means himself. But he is ashamed to say so, and he would have me believe him before a whole Church, that have read the Word of God as well as he. One says one thing, another another; and there is, I say, no measure to end the controversy.' Isn't there? One can at least expose them by pointing out the motives for what they say and do; scepticism at least erodes their claims, hypocrisy and humbug. It is apt also to be a solvent of action: 'if men would say they took arms for anything but religion [or ideology], they might be beaten out of it by reason. Out of that they never can, for they will not believe you whatever you say.' This is good reason for exposing their ideology, eroding their beliefs, their unreason – in the interest of society, which Selden and Hobbes regarded as transcendent.

For once Selden waxes angry at people's illusory beliefs, in speaking of the Trinity. 'The second Person [Christ] is made of a piece of bread by the Papist; the third Person [the Spirit] is made of his own frenzy, malice, ignorance and folly by the Roundhead. One the baker makes, the other the cobbler; and betwixt these two the first Person is sufficiently abused.' It would seem probable that Selden, like Hobbes, was really an undoctrinal deist. He thought that 'the way to find out the truth is by others' mistakings'; if one missed his direction by going too far to the Right, and another to the Left, 'this would direct me to keep the middle way, that peradventure would bring me to the place I desired to go'.

This does not mean that one should not have an eye to

expediency, especially in ill times: both Hobbes and Selden came through theirs, keeping their heads. 'In a troubled state save as much for your own as you can.' One can be too conscientious: 'he that hath a scrupulous conscience is like a horse that is not well wayed: he starts at every bird that flies out of the hedge.' 'Speak not ill of a great enemy, but rather give him good words, that he may use you the better if you chance to fall into his hands.' Both Selden and Hobbes managed to avoid the dangers of the time in which they lived. Neither of them was heroic. But that raises a question of conduct relevant to the time in which we live. How far should resistance to tyranny and terror go? How can it be conducted? It is at least arguable that outer conformity and inner scepticism, in the long run, are more effective and subtler in eroding them than a head-on collision, confirming the terror and eliminating the resistance.

CHAPTER 6

Clarendon versus Hobbes

The most significant criticism of Hobbes, written in the last years of their lives, is that of Clarendon, for he was a man of genius too, if not Hobbes's equal in originality, yet his superior in practical political experience, in knowledge of history and the law, and in counsel. So they were not unequally matched. The confrontation has every kind of interest, chiefly intellectual: it was the historian and politician against the philosopher and analyst. It was that of a concrete mind, thinking in terms of experience, whose method was more empirical, against the theoretical and deductive. Clarendon believed that there was a transcendent, perhaps subconscious, element in politics, one could never be sure how things would work out; and he was a religious man, orthodox and conventional, like Burke sympathetic to tradition and custom. Hobbes was a rationaliser and positivist; he took nothing on trust and believed very little, and like Swift he had little respect for mankind.

A fascinating contrast between their personalities is reflected in their style. Clarendon wrote in long winding sentences, each clause of which bore its weight and had its meaning, sometimes with an ironical sting at the end; often eloquent and appealing, sometimes with a touch of poetry. Hobbes wrote in short and sharp pointed sentences,

157

epigrammatic and paradoxical, intended to provoke and always provoking thought. Clarendon was a rather complacent person. Hobbes was never complacent, though full of self-confidence and well-justified arrogance; his mind – unlike his conduct – was uncompromising, absolute and dogmatic, no room for doubt. It was the middle-of-the-road politician, with a temperate and kindly view of human beings, who courageously suffered for his convictions and was banished the country; Hobbes, who had a low view of human beings, naturally saw to it that he did not suffer at their hands.

A difference of some significance has not been sufficiently marked: Hobbes, as we have seen, was a lower-class man, Clarendon a gentleman with a more hopeful view of men and things.

Edward Hyde was born in 1609 – and so some twenty years Hobbes's junior – also in Wiltshire, but of an old Cheshire family, a country gentleman who bettered himself by two marriages into the upper class. Hyde followed Hobbes at Magdalen Hall, Oxford, and was intended for the Church – this went for something in his make-up, rather clerical and censorious. Later, Hyde and Hobbes became well acquainted with each other and shared the friendship of Falkland and his circle, Ben Jonson, Selden, Waller, Sidney Godolphin – of whom Clarendon wrote, in one of his moving phrases, that he was slain 'by an undiscerned and undiscerning hand'. Though friendly enough, Hobbes and his junior can hardly have been intimate, there was so much in Hobbes that the younger man disapproved of. He was rather a disapproving sort; if the young lawyer was not afraid of telling off Archbishop Laud (who took it well, good man that he was), Hyde, who strongly disapproved of *Leviathan* from the start, did not hesitate to tell Hobbes so. Not content with that, he warned Charles II against it – to whom Hobbes presented the work, grandly engrossed on vellum – and everybody else willing to lend an ear.

6. Clarendon versus Hobbes

It was not until Clarendon was driven into his second and final exile – banished by an ungrateful king – that he found time at length to address himself to the task of confuting Hobbes's book point by point. *A Brief View and Survey of the Dangerous and Pernicious Errors to Church and State in Mr Hobbes's Book, entitled Leviathan* was published at Oxford in 1676. It was prefaced by a pathetic reminder to Charles II of Hobbes's provoking paradox that 'a banished subject, during the banishment, is not a subject; and that a banished man is a lawful enemy of the Commonwealth that banished him, as being no more a member of the same'. Clarendon was a banished man, but as loyal as ever; he signed himself 'one of the oldest Servants that is now living, to your Father and your Self '. He was not even allowed to come home to die. Nothing of that sort happened to Hobbes: his years abroad were of his own choice, he had prudently withdrawn from the approaching war. Clarendon did not fail to reproach him for this piece of wisdom, as again for his return when the coast was clear and the going safe.

Clarendon's book has been much overlooked beside the magnificent bulk of his great *History of the Rebellion* – nor has it the narrative appeal of that, the compulsion of history, the eloquence and poetry, the living portraits of personalities. Naturally enough, for it is a work of (mainly) political thought. Sir Charles Firth's notice of Clarendon in the *Dictionary of National Biography* just gives the title and no more. Properly studied, it gives us the best conspectus of Clarendon's own thinking. It has been criticised for going through *Leviathan* point by point; but I do not see how else it could have been done, and it is effective. Nor is it all that brief – over 320 pages in quarto; it is complete and comprehensive. I find it fascinating, much more so than most books of the time. It is improper to overlook it in any consideration of Clarendon, or indeed of the time.

Controversy in that age was vitriolic and personal (no one more so than Milton, whose life Clarendon helped to save at the Restoration). Clarendon was a more magnanimous man, and did not wish to descend to those depths; however, he gave Hobbes some hard knocks. He often scores, if sometimes with debating points – he was not a lawyer for nothing. Occasionally he makes insinuations, and he continually encourages religious prejudice against Hobbes's exposed front, his rational unbelief. Actually what Clarendon thought his strongest weapon proved his weakest, and exposes him to our way of thinking. Otherwise the contest is not unequal; there is much to be said on both sides, and the confrontation is not without relevance today.

Clarendon, writing in exile at Montpelier in 1670, begins with a generous tribute and some reminiscences of personal interest. 'Mr Hobbes is one of the most ancient acquaintance I have in the world, and of whom I have always had a great esteem as a man who, besides his eminent parts of learning and knowledge, hath been always looked upon as a man of probity, and a life free from scandal. And it may be there are few men now alive who have been longer known to him than I have been in a fair and friendly conversation and sociableness. And I had the honour to introduce those in whose perfections he seemed to take much delight, and whose memory he seems most to extol, first to his acquaintance.' This referred particularly to Sidney Godolphin; and it was from Clarendon while both were in Paris that Hobbes heard of the poet's legacy to him. Clarendon put him in touch with Francis Godolphin, to whom *Leviathan* was dedicated in Sidney's memory.

At the same time Clarendon did not let Hobbes off a few reminders of his mathematical critics, who 'have discovered many gross errors and grosser oversights in those parts of science in which Mr Hobbes would be thought to excel – which are like to put him more out of countenance than anything I can urge against him: by how much he values himself more upon being thought a good philosopher and a good geometrician than a modest man or a good Christian.' A fair score, we may say, if only an *argumentum ad hominem*. Clarendon himself was not a modest man, and was justified in feeling 'not the less competent for those animadversions by the part I had played for many years in the public administration of justice and in the policy of the kingdom'. There follows an insinuation that Cromwell was obliged to support him 'who defended his usurpation', which Clarendon makes more of later. There was no ground for this, since Hobbes returned two years before Cromwell assumed power as Protector. It was just a politician arguing.

The first serious point on which he takes issue is Hobbes's psychology, his reduction of men to an equality, and what men realise when they look into themselves, their fear of pain and death. The practical politician knew quite well that 'much the major part of mankind do not think at all, are not endued with reason enough to opine, or think of what they did last, or what they are to do next, have no reflexion, without which there can be no thinking to this purpose'. Clarendon is right about this, but does it meet the case? Hobbes knew quite as well as Clarendon what fools men are, but he was not engaged in describing them as they are: he was reducing them all to equal atoms, which is all they are from the mass-point of view of society and politics. (Lenin: 'Politics begins with the masses.')

'Death in Mr Hobbes's judgment is equally terrible to all, and with equal care to be avoided or resisted.' Clarendon did not think death the worst of all evils; Hobbes as an unbeliever did, for with him death was the end of everything. Once more the practical politician could say that there were many men who were not frightened of death. Hobbes could reply that they should be, if they had any sense; it was precisely their lack of sense, of any imagination, their inability to foresee the upshot, that brought down upon them the thousands of lives lost in the Civil War – or in our time, the mass-stupidity of the 1930s that led to the holocaust of 1939-1945. Personally Hobbes could decide for himself that the stupidity of those who couldn't see what was coming should not endanger the life of one who did. This was merely a personal conclusion for himself, which he sensibly acted on: he would not endanger his own life out of any sense of community with average humans. To generalise philosophically: was his point of view better conceived from the point of view of the struggle for survival? To live is better than to die – immeasurably better than to *throw* one's life away.

Clarendon had a more optimistic, middle-of-the-road, less extreme view of human nature – which was just as well for a practising politician. God had made man after his own image and in his own likeness, and endowed him with reason; man was made as much for peace as for war, for sociableness as for aggression. This had no force for Hobbes – and indeed such a view was all very well for lucid intervals of tranquillity; but the human record does not consist largely of those. Wars are constantly raging somewhere between human groups, within groups, or between nations and peoples; man is the most aggressive of animals, except possibly panthers – and they do not organise mass-murder. The seventeenth century was filled with wars of every kind, internal and external, civil and national – not then racial; Hobbes, even though writing abstractly and generalising, was reading from man's experience, rightly enough. Clarendon may have been more in keeping with the Victorian age – and indeed there was a Victorian complacency about him – but that was an exceptional period of security in history, and people forget, or do not have the imagination to realise, that it rested on Britain's ascendancy at sea, keeping the ring world-wise. Hobbes's view is more in keeping with the catastrophic twentieth century.

Moreover, there is a certain insularity in Clarendon's point of view – and the English Civil War was at least more gentlemanly than the horrors of the Thirty Years' War that devastated Germany. Hobbes thought that with primitive original man 'the notions of right and wrong have no place, but Force and Fraud are the two cardinal virtues; that there is no property, no dominion, no mine or thine distinct, but only that to be every man's that he can get, and for so long as he can keep it'. This was un-English of him, and rather shocking to English readers; Clarendon was very English, and shockable. Hobbes was more European; or, we might say, had a world view, in keeping with world history.

We must allow that some advantage attached to Clarendon's insular point of view: it gave him faith that, after the Puritan Revolution had exhausted itself, things would come round again. He had confidence in the longer-term processes of history and in the eventual sense of the English people. In 1646 he was hoping for 'the resurrection of the English loyalty and courage' (he had to go on hoping for fourteen years), and placed his hopes in the natural affections for native air, soil, inhabitants than 'any abstracted notions of good and bad, right and wrong, true and false'.[1] Hobbes had no such confidence, and even Clarendon allowed that to escape being deceived during these bad years would have required a disposition too uncharitable and distrustful. But, surely, the facts warranted distrust. Clarendon admitted that going by votes, and plurality of voices, gave 'no security for what is last concluded'; though, if the votes of the people in general had been consulted, the monarchy would have been restored long before 1660. Clarendon's confidence was justified that 'a firm peace can never be established but by the old [constitution]'. He was a constitutionalist, a traditionalist; Hobbes not.

[1] Cf. B.H.G. Wormald, *Clarendon*, 172, 181, 196.

As a philosopher Hobbes was generalising. Once more Clarendon objected to his view that 'every man must acknowledge every other man for his equal'. Clarendon agreed with Aristotle that 'by nature some are fit to command, and others to serve'. Even among horses, 'some by nature are fitter for nobler uses, others to be only beasts of burden' – and there is far greater variation in quality in man than in any other animal. Clarendon quoted the Bible, Solomon against Hobbes, 'The foolish man shall be the servant of the wise.' One wonders what Hobbes would think of this, when he himself, the wise man, was a servant of a waster in the second Earl of Devonshire. No wonder he was apt to reverse the sense of Holy Writ. 'Divine Providence doth show and demonstrate who are fit and proper for low and vile offices, not only by very notable defects in their understandings, incapable of any cultivation, which makes them unfit to bear rule. ... Nature itself hath a bounty which extends to some men in a much superior degree than she doth to others.' Hobbes knew all this as well as Clarendon; it would not affect his fundamental proposition that men were equal in their essential human nature as such, to which he was reducing them, as he reduced everything to its simplest elements for his constructions. He was an analyst, not an historian or practical politician.

His construction of an absolute sovereign, of authoritarian rule, is based on the view that humans, of their essential nature, are so aggressive and predatory that without it there would be anarchy. The relevance of this today may be seen from what has happened in Russian history when autocracy has broken down: anarchy, followed by dictatorship, as after the French Revolution; or, for that matter, with Cromwell in England. Hobbes was not so far out as English liberals have always thought; his view of human nature was truer than their illusions about it.

Clarendon would not have it that sovereignty derived

from the people, Hobbes's elemental atoms; he held a more traditional, sacramental view, touching for the King's Evil and all that. (That went out only with the Hanoverians, after Clarendon's grand-daughter, Queen Anne, who 'touched' Dr Johnson as a boy. It didn't do him any good.) To Hobbes nothing was sacred: his construction was 'a government that he would himself like to be trusted with, having determined liberty, property and religion to be only empty words, and to have no other existence than in the will and breast of this sovereign governor. And all this in order to make his people happy, and to enjoy the blessing of peace.' And what better? Hobbes could reply; or, with Lenin, 'Liberty? What for?' Even the facts would show that the masses prefer security, material objects and gadgets, than the liberty so much desiderated by middle-class dissidents. Hobbes's inflexion was more in keeping with lower-class options, as later against upper-class conceptions of honour: he thought survival more important.

Hobbes's conception of a fundamental contract upon which society is based, for the sake of security and self-preservation, is an abstract one, founded on necessity. He did not think of it in historical or anthropological terms, as Locke more nearly did, who was interested in primitive societies. To Hobbes it was necessity, a kind of compact at the root of men coming together to form groups; otherwise – anarchy, chaos. It is a contract to erect sovereign power, certainly not a contract between sovereign and people (as Locke and the Whigs were to put forward). Still less was it a covenant of the people with God – Hobbes had seen too much of those claims with the egregious Covenant of the Presbyterian Scots. Hobbes said shortly that 'the pretence of Covenant with God is so evident a lie, even in the pretenders' own consciences'. This was true enough of aristocratic Scotch politicians who, for their own purposes, took the lead of the rebellion instigated by the ministers, whatever the people believed.

Clarendon answered, as a moderate, that the sovereign might admit limitations on his power without sovereignty breaking down. He argues effectively – with a flout that Hobbes might have been informed as to the facts, 'if he had been so modest as to think he had need of any information' – that if he 'had known anything of the constitution of the monarchy of England ... he could never have thought that the late troubles there proceeded from an opinion received of the greatest part of England that "the power was divided between the King, and the Lords, and the House of Commons".' Clarendon said that this revolutionary view was never heard of till the rebellion began, and was clean contrary to law and historical tradition.

Here Clarendon was on strong ground as both eminent lawyer and a practical politician who had played a leading rôle throughout the crisis. He dismisses Hobbes's view with the remark, 'his extraordinary and notorious ignorance in the laws and constitution of the government of England makes him a very incompetent judge and informer of the cause or original of the late woeful calamities in England, of which he knows no more than every other man of Malmesbury doth'. Here is the usual superciliousness of the politician-in-the-know at the outside observer looking on. But who sees most of the game? In this case the observer had the sharpest eyes in England, with the advantage of a European perspective, and no upper-class illusions. Clarendon, like all politicians, interpreted political events in personal terms, without probing into the deeper causes and forces that shape events and play games with the men who think they are directing them.

Clarendon had good fun, as a lawyer, in laughing at Hobbes's notion of the laws. 'The opinions and judgments which are found in the books of eminent lawyers cannot be answered and controlled [i.e. criticised] by Mr Hobbes's wonder, since the men who know least are apt to wonder most.' Hobbes was legislating 'without so much as considering what is law here or there, but by the general notions he hath of law and what it is by long study and much cogitation.' Clarendon appeals to the authority of the lawyers on the matter at issue: 'methinks if that be the judgment of eminent lawyers, Mr Hobbes should be so modest as to believe it to be true, till he hears others as eminent declare the contrary.' They 'must be understood to be more competent for that determination than Mr Hobbes can be for the alteration of law and government by the artificial reason he hath attained to by long study of arithmetic and geometry'.

But neither lawyers nor anybody else – least of all ecclesiastics or theologians – had any authority for Thomas Hobbes. He could have answered, even factually and historically, hadn't they all together made a mess of things? Clarendon may have known that Hobbes had written his historical work, *Behemoth*, going into the facts and events leading to the Civil War. This was not here the intellectual point at issue, though Hobbes was quite prepared to confute the sacred bull of English law, Chief Justice Coke, on the common law, where he was regarded as a sanctified prophet. Nothing sacred to Hobbes. He had the sublime confidence to probe into the essence of law as he probed into the essence of everything, with his weapons of definition and deduction.

Here is the crux of the difference between Clarendon and Hobbes, a difference of method and approach, between the historian and the philosopher, between inductive observation – which Hobbes thought little of, he said that no *general* conclusions could be based upon it – and rigorous analysis. At one point Clarendon put his finger on it when he said reproachfully, 'if Mr Hobbes had thought fit to write problematically and to have examined the nature of government and the nature of mankind that is to be governed, and from the conclusion of both had modestly proposed such a form as to his judgment might better provide for the security, peace and happiness of a people, which is the end of government' ... then Hobbes would have done better than he had done in *Leviathan*.

Clarendon has here a strong case. When he said that Hobbes should consider questions of government 'problematically', Clarendon meant what we should call 'pragmatically', which is what a politician would think. But this had no authority with Hobbes: he wanted to get down to the essence of the matter, the essentials of government, the underlying necessities and exigencies of society. Clarendon thought these mere speculations, and 'truly, if he would rectify his speculations, that is, his conceptions and imaginations by examining those of other men – a fatal neglect he hath been guilty of throughout his whole life ...'. But other men's opinions, muddled and confused as Hobbes pointed them out to be, had no more authority for him than texts of Scripture, of which he took delight in exposing the contradictions and confusions, and ordinary people's ridiculous interpretations of them, only leading to trouble.

Which of them was more true to the essence of the matter, the nature of man? Hobbes's groundwork was that 'war is founded in nature, which gives the stronger a right to whatever the weaker is possessed of; so that there can be no peace or security from oppression till such covenants are made as may appoint a sovereign to have all that power which is necessary to provide for that peace and security'. Whereas, Clarendon contradicts, 'we say that peace is founded in nature, and that when the God of nature gave his creature, Man, dominion ... he gave him natural strength and power to govern the world with peace and order'. And Clarendon, as a religious believer, goes back to argue the matter in terms of the Bible, the peaceful dominion under Adam and Seth and so on – nothing is said about Cain's murder of Abel: perhaps we might regard that as a metaphor for the existence of both war and peace from the beginning.

6. *Clarendon versus Hobbes*

Clarendon confessed himself 'very unwilling to enter the lists with Mr Hobbes upon the interpretation of Scriptures, which he handles as imperiously as he doth a text of Aristotle, putting such unnatural interpretation on the words and drawing very unnatural inferences from them'. Hobbes had indeed, sailing close to the wind, had a great deal of fun in this way all through *Leviathan*, and in drawing out improprieties from the text. The sacredness of property? What about our Saviour's example when he commanded his disciples to take away the man's ass to carry him into Jerusalem – and the man 'did not ask whether his necessity was a sufficient title, nor whether he was a judge of that necessity, but did acquiesce in the will of the Lord', i.e. an exercise of unquestioned sovereignty. Or what about the Prophet Samuel's declaration that when the Chosen People entered Canaan they should have a king set over them? Clarendon was forced to admit it reasonable to deduce an 'absolute and illimited power of kings from that declaration by Samuel [Deuteronomy 17], which indeed seems to leave neither property or liberty in their subjects'.

The seventeenth century argued these issues in Biblical terms: their interest for us is anthropological. Modern psychology would seem to agree with anthropology and history that man is essentially an aggressive animal – and in a nuclear world has discovered the capacity to destroy mankind and devastate the planet. Which had the truer view, the deeper, more universal vision – Clarendon or Hobbes? Hobbes's view would seem to cover the facts of international conflict more convincingly. As for internal peace, security and order, is it likely that the collapse of authority in Russia or China would lead to them?

Clarendon doffs his hat to Hobbes in passing, to 'the authority of his name and the pleasantness of his style', but does not think well of the logic of his discourse. We may think that Hobbes was the more exact logician, and

169

Clarendon misses Hobbes's technical point, namely that from any amount of inductive considerations one could not draw general conclusions that were certain. The historian was much against the geometrical mind, and shocked at Hobbes's deductions from first principles. 'He doth not profess to be a strict casuist, nor can he be a good observer of the rules of moral honesty ... nor is he in truth a competent judge of the most enormous crimes when he reckons "theft, adultery, sodomy and any other vice that may be taken for an effect of power or a cause of pleasure, to be of such a nature as amongst men are to be taken against law, rather than against honour".' One sees how Hobbes would appeal later to the Utilitarians, with their pleasure-pain calculus.

He was a positivist and something of a nominalist. Clarendon constantly complains that Hobbes empties words of their content – liberty, justice, honour and so on. We can appreciate that often he is emptying them of their humbug; he loves to point out how people's professions differ from their practice, and that words on ordinary people's lips often have no meaning, while faith is simply not worth discussing – people will believe anything, and prefer nonsense to sense. It is a historian, Lecky, who points out that men will believe anything in spite of the evidence, often contrary to the evidence, but hardly ever on account of the evidence. Clarendon as historian, politician and lawyer should have known that: it is odd that he had a more optimistic view, in spite of his own experience. He was sustained by faith – as he would need to be to survive as a politician: a vocational inflexion. We can conclude so far that even the facts spoke as much for the detached observer as for the practical politician.

Hobbes was at a disadvantage in not being able to speak out all that he thought, surrounded as he was by religious believers. Even so, he got away with a lot. He said that much of people's discourse 'may be numbered amongst the sorts of madness, namely when men speak such words as, put together, have in them no signification at all'. Often words had little force for people who had them on their lips. Clarendon was put out by Hobbes attaching little significance to concepts like honour, obligation, duty. The contrast here between the two contains a class-element: these notions were more important in Clarendon's mind as an upper-class man, for they are the concepts of the civilised elect who give them what consequence they have in a society directed by them.

We recall Falstaff on the subject, who had no chivalrous illusions. 'Honour pricks me on. How then? Can honour set to a leg? – No. Or an arm? – No. Or take away the grief of a wound? – No. Honour hath no skill in surgery then? – No. What is honour? – A word. What is that word "honour"? – Air. Who hath it? – He that died o' Wednesday. Doth he feel it? – No. Doth he hear it? – No. It is insensible then? – Yea, to the dead ... Therefore I'll none of it: honour is a mere scutcheon', i.e. a decoration, an 'honour'. Hobbes thought as Falstaff did. Clarendon was scornful of Hobbes's fear of death, and 'his precious bodily fear of corporal hurt'. But to Hobbes, survival was what mattered, and in his time the lives of many good men were thrown away – to what point? And what about our catastrophic time?

We may conclude that Hobbes's view of society was grounded in his sense of man's struggle for survival – in this a deeper and more universal grasp than Clarendon's.

Clarendon had the limitations as well as the strengths of the historical approach. He reproves Hobbes for his 'so great a prejudice to the reading of histories – as if they were all enemies to his government', and laughs at his taking 'so much delight in reiterating the many ill things he hath said, for fear they do not make impression deep enough in the minds of men'. There is a pleasure in that, as well as the necessity in denting the brains of numbskulls.

Clarendon was too good a historian to subscribe to the

myth against the Norman Conquest which ran riot among the Levellers, ideologues and radicals down to Cobbett and on to Chesterton. But Clarendon himself was under some illusions about the continuity of English with Anglo-Saxon institutions. Naturally much of his historical excursus is out of date and superseded. Hobbes's views do not suffer from that disadvantage.

Still less in the sphere of religion: where Clarendon fancied himself strongest he was really at his weakest; where his conventional orthodoxy had most appeal at the time he is now exploded. He was, for example, tethered to the sacrosanct authority of the Bible. Hobbes, the rationalist, dared to place it in the same scales as the Koran. He went so far as to say that 'Moses was not the author of the Five Books which the Christian world generally believe to be written by him'. Nor was he; it was very original of Hobbes to realise it at that time, but again he had the advantage of not subscribing to nonsense-beliefs.

As for the Old Testament Prophets, Hobbes must have taken delight in what offended Clarendon, that a prophet 'sometimes signifies a foreteller of things to come, and sometimes one that speaketh incoherently, as men that are distracted'. He had plenty of opportunity to observe the type among the Puritans, not only in their lunatic fringe of Fifth Monarchy men, Millenarians, Soul-Sleepers, Muggletonians and such. It was deplorable that Hobbes should be 'content that the heathen poets shall likewise be called prophets' – from which we may infer that Hobbes had a glimpse of what would become the study of comparative religion. He had suggested that what these creatures said came from dreams and apparitions, 'from the imagination which they had in their sleep or in ecstasy'.

As for their teachings and their miracles Hobbes was content that the sovereign power should determine what was to be believed. After all, 'he preserves to himself and other private men the prerogative of believing or not believing in his heart, because thought is free'. They were not however to contradict the official doctrine openly – so much for dissidents. A deeper question opens up here. One may well think that so sceptical an attitude would be more effective in eroding the nonsense of official doctrine than openly challenging it – with the latter positions are taken up and people entrench themselves in mutually conflicting 'convictions'. It is arguable that the sceptical, though conformist, attitude of an Erasmus would gradually sap and undermine the positive and persecuting nonsense of Catholics and Protestants on either side of the Reformation. The Reformation strengthened mutually exclusive beliefs, which gave people an excuse to fight and encouraged them to it. The scepticism and ambivalent conformism of a Montaigne would have made the Thirty Years' War less likely.

Hobbes continued to have fun with miracles – Clarendon deplored that 'he hath a mind to lessen the faith of the greatest miracles which have been wrought'. Hobbes must have had his tongue in his cheek when he wrote that 'the works of the Egyptian sorcerers, though not as great as those of Moses, were yet great miracles'. He added, with poker-face, that 'a miracle was the work of God (besides his operation by the way of nature ordained in the creation) done for the making manifest to his elect the mission of an extraordinary minister for their salvation'. He then explained that 'the magicians of Egypt were impostors and did no great matter; for when the rod seemed a serpent or the waters blood ... nor the rod nor the water was enchanted, but the spectator. So that the miracle consisted only in this, that the enchanter had deceived a man – which is no miracle.' We perceive that he was at one with Hume and Gibbon on miracles.

Clarendon well understood Hobbes's irony, which escaped ordinary intelligences and allowed him to get away with so much – 'the bare-faced denying the Trinity might naturally have followed, which he makes to be no mystery at all.' Over religion Clarendon gets more and more infuriated with Hobbes, and twice suggests that the governors of the Church, both in England and abroad – who have 'permitted it to receive too much countenance in Popish countries likewise' – should not have allowed it to be printed, i.e. censor when you can't answer. Then there was Hobbes's provocative way of quoting Scripture for his own naughty purpose: 'profession with the tongue is but an external thing, wherein a Christian holding firmly in his heart the faith of Christ, hath the same liberty which the Prophet Elisha allowed to Naaman the Syrian.' The prophet, we remember, allowed him to bow down in the heathen house of Rimmon.

Mr Hobbes didn't think much of martyrs. It was of no use to quote to him the example of the 'many hundred thousand lives of the Christians in the primitive persecution, when the greatest part of them were not required with their mouth to deny Jesus Christ', but simply to be polite to Jupiter or Venus or Apollo. Hobbes held the simple view that it would have been better to be polite and save the lives of thousands. Clarendon quoted Seneca at him about its not mattering whether one died sooner or later, so long as one escaped the danger of living ill – but he committed suicide by opening his veins in a bath, which Mr Hobbes would not at all have fancied. Clarendon then threw Daniel at him, 'who chose to be thrown into the hot fiery furnace, rather than to fall down before the image which Nebuchednezer had set up'. All to no good: the incorrigible philosopher thought it 'a sin only in men whose actions are looked at by others as lights to guide them by, whereas the example of those we regard not works not upon us at all'. I cannot forbear to cheer: the elect do not choose to live their lives in the light of other people's eyes, conforming to the standards thought proper by people whose intelligence they despise. The elect should make the rules, or at least live by their own.

What are martyrs? A martyr signifies a witness, 'and a witness must have seen what he testifies. Therefore none can properly be called martyrs of Christ but those that conversed with him, and saw him before and after his resurrection. Whosoever did not so can witness no more than what others said and are therefore but witnesses of other men's testimony.' We can draw our own conclusions as to the value of other people's testimony; the elect know that no two ordinary people can tell the tale alike, they can hardly ever tell one the colour of another person's eyes. So much, it is implied, for the witnesses of resurrection, ascension, etc.

Now for preaching. Preaching signifies nothing 'but what a crier or herald useth to do publicly, and a crier hath not right to command any man. Teaching is the same thing with preaching, but to teach that Jesus was Christ and risen from the dead is not to say that men are bound, after they believe it, to obey them that tell them so against the commands of their sovereign.' Then, with tongue in cheek, Hobbes bids them 'to expect the coming of Christ hereafter in patience and faith, with obedience to their present magistrate'. Obedience is the operative word – what is good for ordinary people. So much for all the preaching fanatics who proliferated with Puritanism, in particular the millenarians and idiot sects who at that time expected – as Major General Harrison, the regicide, did – the imminent coming of Christ. Milton, at one time, was not far off from expecting it, but encountered the Restoration of the ungodly Charles II instead.

'Baptism in the name of the Father, and of the Son, and of the Holy Ghost, is dipping in their names' – 'you shall rarely find him call them three Persons,' Clarendon points out, and adds, 'he tells us often that Spirit signifies nothing but mind.' Clarendon waxes really angry now. 'In all these

175

ravings we have texts of Scripture at hand, which he perverts and interprets to his own ends, contrary to the whole analogy of faith and the interpretation which hath been always made of them before Mr Hobbes.' That had no authority for Mr Hobbes. Clarendon concluded that this 'clearly absolves the Jews for not believing our Saviour himself when he alleged texts of Scripture to inform and convince them'. One civilised aspect of Cromwell's policy was the re-admission of the Jews into England: it never occurred to conventional people like Clarendon that *their* interpretation of these matters would give a more rational account of them and, apart from some natural bias, offer a better guide to what actually happened.

Clarendon could fall back only on faith, and angry rhetoric. 'It is a very painful thing to read all the loose and licentious reflections upon piety and religion, and undervaluing and perverting the Scripture, and the utter contempt of the Church [Hobbes was no aesthete – my one charge against him], which are a little more warily scattered throughout his book – that is, by being scattered, not so easily discerned – are collected into such a mass of impiety', in Chapter 42, 'Of Power Ecclesiastical'. To Hobbes this was the fount of much evil and he fairly let himself go.

Chapter 43 is even naughtier, under the provoking title, 'Of What is necessary for a Man's Reception into the Kingdom of Heaven'. It did not appear that much was necessary – and on the other hand Hobbes did not believe in Hell-fire. This chapter is even more sceptical, and asks questions which Clarendon cannot answer. 'The most ordinary immediate cause of our belief, concerning any point of Christian faith, is that we believe the Bible to be the word of God. But why we believe the Bible to be the word of God is much disputed – as all questions must be that are not well stated.' And then, with a contemporary reflexion upon all the preposterous preachers presumptuously pretending to lay down the law – 'how shall a man know his own private

176

spirit to be other than a belief, grounded upon the authority and arguments of his teachers; or upon a presumption of his own gifts?' And then, 'it is manifest therefore that Christian men do not know, but only believe the Scripture to be the word of God; and that the means of making them believe is according to the way of nature, that is to say from their teachers'. He asks the sceptical question, 'but if teaching be the cause of faith, why do not all believe?'; and 'what other cause can there be assigned why in Christian commonwealths all men either believe, or at least profess, the Scripture to be the word of God, and in other commonwealths scarce any – but that in Christian commonwealths they are taught it from their infancy, *and in other places they are taught otherwise?*' In other words, men simply believe in accordance with the beliefs that prevail in the places where they are brought up. Once more we see Hobbes in keeping with facts – men in fact do conform. Hobbes's is a world view, where Clarendon's is insular and Anglican.

With tongue in cheek Hobbes had said, 'nor is it any shame to confess the profoundness of the Scripture to be too great to be sounded by the shortness of human understanding', and then goes on to show up its incredibilities. As to the Devil taking Christ up into a mountain to tempt him with the whole world, 'there is not any mountain high enough to show him one whole hemisphere', he says with his regular literalness of mind. (Milton did better to turn it into poetry, as the myth it was.) Clarendon was shocked that Hobbes regarded the whole episode and 'all that relates thereunto to be nothing else but a vision or dream – than which no Jew could more undervalue it, or Christ be more dishonoured than to have his conflict with the enemy of mankind to be looked on only and considered as a dream'. I fear that Clarendon had no understanding of the rôle of myth in human history, as a historian should have.

Nor would Hobbes believe that 'our Saviour ever cast the Devil out of any man, only that he cured those persons of madness or lunacy – which cures have been wrought by many other persons, and so unworthy to be reckoned amongst the miracles of Christ'. Nor did he believe that Satan entered into Judas: 'I wonder he doth not impute his hanging himself afterwards to nothing but a fit of melancholy.' We see that Hobbes is the better psychologist, as he was anthropologist. Clarendon ends up furious at Hobbes's paradoxes about religion and sums them up – such as 'none can know that the Scriptures are God's word (though all true Christians believe it), but they to whom God himself hath revealed it supernaturally'. That means, to Hobbes, not at all – a mere delusion; he implies therefore that Christians are foolish to believe it. 'By the kingdom of heaven is meant the kingdom of the king that dwelleth in heaven', i.e. no-where. 'The immortal life beginneth not in man till the resurrection and day of judgment, and hath for cause, not his specifical nature and generation, but promise.' That is, not natural fact, but illusion – as Pius XII declared in promulgating the doctrine of the bodily Assumption of the Virgin Mary into heaven, it was not a terrestrial fact, but a celestial fact, i.e. not one at all.

In truth Hobbes did not hesitate to define 'religion to be fear of power invisible, feigned by the mind, or imagined from tales publicly told'; he considered that it grew from 'opinion of ghosts, ignorance of second causes, devotion to what men fear, and taking things casual for prognostics'. And ordinary people are such fools that, as Aubrey tells us, they believed that Hobbes was 'afraid to lie alone at night in his chamber'. Hobbes told Aubrey, with his usual down-to-earth common sense that 'he was not afraid of sprites, but afraid of being knocked on the head for £5 or £10, which rogues might think he had in his chamber'. Much more in keeping with his view of humans.

Clarendon ended with personal reflexions: 'I never read

any book that contains in it so much sedition, treason and impiety as this *Leviathan*; and therefore it is very unfit to be read, taught or sold.' He thought that it should be condemned by sovereign authority and publicly burned. Though this was not done (Charles II agreed with most of it) we have seen that Hobbes's works were censored and those dealing with political or social thought not allowed to appear. Clarendon admits that nothing could be done with the impenitent thinker: 'what kind of arguments to apply towards the information or conversion of him is very difficult to find. That which is got by reasoning from the authority of books will work nothing upon him, *"because it is not knowledge but faith"*.' It did not occur to the complacent Clarendon that it is impertinent to suggest to a person of superior intellect that he should follow the opinions of one inferior.

They did succeed in driving Hobbes underground, and shortly, with the Revolution of 1688, there prevailed the moderate, middle-of-the-road philosophic outlook of Locke, which was much more in keeping with the temperate English tradition and dominated in various forms the next two centuries of English complacency – well justified by the achievements of their governing class. With the decline and break-up of all that, in our calamitous time, we can see that the plebeian Hobbes saw deeper into human nature and is now more in keeping with the facts.[2]

Clarendon was beyond doing Hobbes any personal harm. He ended, as he began, with 'the profession of so much esteem for his parts, and reverence for his very vigorous age, which in and for itself is venerable'. When Clarendon's

---

[2] As for Hobbes's moral philosophy, our leading authority today – after an immensely scholastic inquisition into it – sums up simply, 'his conclusion remains deeply sceptical, and does little to uphold the dignity of moral philosophy. For all that, however, he may well be right.' (Quentin Skinner, 'Thomas Hobbes: Rhetoric and the Construction of Morality', *Proceedings of the British Academy*, vol. 76, p. 56).

book came out in 1676 – in itself a remarkable piece of work, from a great man – he was already dead by a couple of years. Hobbes, twenty years older, had three more years of hale and hearty life. Clarendon said that he would have been glad enough for Hobbes to have had to endure the burden and toil of practical politics, as against his retired life 'in his quiet quarter in the Peak, without envy of those whom he left in employment, rather than keep them longer company in so toilsome, uneasy and ungrateful transactions'.

It is true that Clarendon had borne, and suffered, from the heat and burden of the day; but he was a member of the governing class, and had got on with it. He had his reward, for the price he paid: his peerage and fortune and fame, a noble family to continue his line, his daughter married to the heir to the throne, his grand-daughter Queen of England; perhaps better still, his name carried on in the institutions of the university of Oxford. Hobbes was a solitary man, no family or hostages to fortune, having nothing but his genius to declare, a light shining over the dark and murderous waters that threaten to engulf us.

Index

Index